A Good and Faithful Servant

The Year of Saint Innocent

An exhibit commemorating the bicentennial of the birth of Ioann Veniaminov 1797–1997

University of Alaska Fairbanks
& Alaska State Veniaminov Bicentennial Committee
1997

All dates are in the Julian calendar. To convert to the Gregorian (modern) calendar, add 12 days to the 19th-century dates.

Exhibit staff:
Robert C. Banghart & Associates, exhibit designers, Douglas, Alaska
Bruce H. Kato, Chief Curator, Alaska State Museums, Juneau, Alaska
Mark Daughhetee, Curator of Exhibitions, Alaska State Museum, Juneau, Alaska
Peter L. Corey, Curator of Collections, Sheldon Jackson Museum, Sitka, Alaska

Catalog:
Edited by Lydia Black, assisted by Katherine L. Arndt.
Designed by Dixon J. Jones, AMS Graphics, UAF Rasmuson Library. Prepress assistance by Rose Tomasulo.
Genealogical chart compiled by James W. Cook.
Base map for inside front cover by Martin Gutoski.
Front cover icon of St. Innocent by Courtenay Birdsall.
Back cover icon of St. Innocent by Byron Birdsall.

Elmer E. Rasmuson Library cataloging-in-publication:

A good and faithful servant : the year of Saint Innocent : an exhibit commemorating the bicentennial of the birth of Ioann Veniaminov, 1797–1997 / edited by Lydia Black ; assisted by Katherine L. Arndt.

1. Innokentiĭ, Saint, Metropolitan of Moscow and Kolomna, 1797–1879––Exhibitions. I. Black, Lydia. II. Arndt, Katherine L. III. University of Alaska Fairbanks. IV. Alaska State Veniaminov Bicentennial Committee.

BX597.I55G66 1997

Contents

STATE OF ALASKA

Executive Proclamation
by
Tony Knowles, Governor

1997 marks the bicentennial of the birth of Ioann (John) Veniaminov, the distinguished Russian Orthodox missionary, teacher, administrator, linguist, ethnographer, and architect. John Veniaminov served as the first priest at Unalaska, the first Orthodox bishop in Alaska, and head of the Orthodox Church of Russia. In 1977 he was canonized a saint, St. Innocent, Apostle to North America and Siberia.

Communities throughout the United States, Russia, and England are observing Veniaminov's contributions to Alaskan, Russian, and American history by presenting exhibitions and conferences, and the publishing of new books of his writings. Such observances will be prominent in Alaska where Veniaminov served as missionary priest and bishop from 1825 through 1852. A major exhibition featuring the life and legacy of Veniaminov will travel to many communities in the state.

John Veniaminov (Bishop Innocent) is honored by Alaska Natives for his dedication to preserving Native languages, for his development of the Aleut orthography, for many translations into Aleut, and for his pioneering development of a Tlingit Alphabet. He is also honored as a teacher, founder of the first school at Unalaska and of the first Orthodox school, seminary, and orphanage at Sitka.

John Veniaminov was an accomplished builder, having designed and constructed the National Historic Landmark Cathedral of St. Michael in Sitka. He also built the first Church of the Holy Ascension at Unalaska. State, federal, and private monies are presently restoring this National Historic Landmark which contains many of the architectural features from the original church of 1825.

The occasion of the rededication of the historic Unalaska church is an appropriate time to proclaim the Veniaminov Bicentennial.

NOW, THEREFORE, I, Tony Knowles, Governor of the State of Alaska, do hereby proclaim 1997,

The Veniaminov Bicentennial Year

in Alaska, and encourage all Alaskans to join in recognizing the contributions to Alaska of this great Russian missionary, scholar, and statesman.

DATED: September 9, 1996

THE SEAL OF THE STATE OF ALASKA

Tony Knowles, Governor
who has also authorized the seal
of the State of Alaska
to be affixed to this proclamation.

With an affirmative vision for the peoples of northeastern Asia and Alaska and their ancestral cultures, and with cooperative interactions there, St. Innocent of Alaska and Siberia (formerly Father Ioann Veniaminov) provided leadership for constructive transition during times of international contact and change.

–Soterios A. Mousalimas, Program of the International Symposium to Commemorate the Bicentennial of the Birth of Innokentii Veniaminov, Pembroke College, Oxford University, 14–15 April 1997

The log cabin in which St. Innocent was born in the village of Anga, near Irkutsk, Russia.

Photo by Vladimir Guliaev, courtesy of Oleg V. Bychkov.

:I: The Early Years

St. Innocent was born Ivan (Ioann) Popov, one of the four children and the eldest son of Evsevii (Evsei) Popov and his wife, Fekla. The Popovs resided in the village of Anga, a seventeenth-century Russian settlement on the upper Lena River near the City of Irkutsk (founded in 1661), in Buriatia. Not far from the village were numerous homesteads of the Mongolian-speaking Buriat, whose religious life encompassed complex shamanic practices and among whom Lamaist Buddhism was gaining ascendancy.

Very little is known about the family's origins and how and when they came to settle in Buriatia, except that, like the majority of Russian settlers in Siberia, they were from the Pomor'ie—the arctic seas littoral of European Russia. It is stated that the family was of peasant origin, but the surname (Popov) suggests that at some point an ancestor in the male line entered the clerical estate.[1] In any case, they were devoutly Orthodox and had numerous ties to the Church. Evsevii was sacristan of the Church of St. Elias in his home village of Anga. Evsevii's brother Dimitrii was deacon in the same church. Widowed, Dimitrii took monastic vows, assuming the name of David, became a priest-monk (hieromonk), and was assigned to the bishop's see in Irkutsk. His son, Dimitrii Popov, also served the Church. He died in 1799 in the wreck of the *Phoenix*, on the way to Kodiak, together with Bishop Ioasaf and his retinue. He was a chorister and member of the bishop's staff.[2] All his life St. Innocent regularly made offerings for commemoration of his numerous relatives who were churchmen.

The family was poor. The log cabin in which St. Innocent was born survives and is an eloquent testimony to that fact. When Evsevii died in 1803 at the age of thirty-nine years, his widow and four children found themselves in desperate straits. St. Innocent's biographer, Ivan Barsukov, states that when little Ivan read the gospel in the church, he was clad in a collarless

The City of Irkutsk, Russia.
Photo by Vladimir Guliaev, courtesy of Oleg V. Bychkov.

peasant homespun work coat and homemade Siberian working boots. In later life, St. Innocent was moved to write an essay about his childhood in Anga, but this work, together with his account of his first journey from Irkutsk to Alaska, was lost in 1858 when the fire that broke out in the Savior Monastery in Yakutsk engulfed his cell.

Poor as the family was, the children were given the best education it could provide. Ioann was effectively home schooled, first by his ailing father, then by his uncle Dimitrii. At the age of nine, in 1806, he was brought to Irkutsk and entered the seminary, where he spent almost eleven years. His younger brother Stephan did not make the grade and attended the city school. Ioann, on the other hand, proved to be exceptionally gifted intellectually, in manual skills, and musically.

Hieromonk David kept a close eye on his nephews. While unable to help the boys much in material terms (the years in the seminary were lean years, indeed), he provided guidance and taught them a number of skills. Both Ioann and Stephan became excellent carpenters and joiners. Ioann also learned metal work and precision instrument making from his uncle, a

Irkutsk Seminary.
Photo by Vladimir Guliaev, courtesy of Oleg V. Bychkov.

gifted master mechanic. While still in Irkutsk, he made furniture, clocks, and musical instruments, and constructed his first organ. Later, he sold the organs he made to earn some extra income, both in Irkutsk and in Alaska. He received additional training in clock making from a master-specialist, experimented with various inventions in time-keeping mechanisms, and later was so skilled that he often repaired and adjusted chronometers on naval vessels that called at Sitka, both Russian and British. He enjoyed manual work very much and almost to the very end of his life spent some time every day in his workshop: in Unalaska, in Sitka, in Blagoveshchensk.

When Ioann graduated from the Irkutsk Seminary in 1817, his mentors expected him to continue his ecclesiastical education at the Spiritual Academy in St. Petersburg. Ioann, however, took matters into his own hands and, before his elders could interfere, married a young woman his own age, a priest's daughter, Ekaterina (Catherine) Sharin.[3] We have no pictures of Ekaterina, but it was apparently a love match and we should like to think of her as an intelligent and attractive woman. Ioann was devoted to her.

The Church of the Annunciation in Irkutsk.

Photo by Vladimir Guliaev, courtesy of Oleg V. Bychkov.

With the academy in the distant imperial capital now out of the question, Ioann Popov was assigned as a deacon to the Church of the Annunciation in Irkutsk. Here, young Deacon Ioann built offering tables and candle stands for his church, taught children in a sort of Sunday school he initiated, taught in the parish school, and gave instruction in music at the seminary. He conceived a scheme for universal early education, for both boys and girls, which he presented to his bishop. Though the bishop approved the project, other priests in Irkutsk evidenced little enthusiasm for it. Only in Alaska would Ioann be able to create schools on the model he envisioned as a young cleric/teacher.

Popular with his parishioners, and approved by his superiors, in 1821 Ioann Popov was consecrated priest. It was on this occasion that Bishop Michael of Irkutsk[4] bestowed on Ioann Popov a new surname—Veniaminov—to honor the much beloved late Bishop Veniamin (Benjamin).[5] From then on, Ioann Veniaminov and his family, including his brother Stephan and all their descendants, would be known under this surname.

Notes

1 From the time of Peter the Great, Russian society was based on a system of hereditary (in the male line) ranked estates, each rank having specific rights and duties and obligations to the state. Clerics and their families constituted a separate estate implicitly outside the rank system. However, through service to the state, individuals could enter higher ranks and in most cases such an achieved higher rank became hereditary.

2 This information comes from a footnote in St. Innocent's *Notes on the Islands of the Unalashka District.* See English-language edition by R.A. Pierce (Kingston, Ontario: The Limestone Press, 1984), 236.

3 Her father, Ioann Sharin, later became a much-venerated monk at the Savior Monastery in Yakutsk.

4 Mikhail Burdukov, Bishop of Irkutsk 1814-1826, Archbishop 1826-1830, cited after O.E. Naumova, *Irkutskaia eparkhiia XVII-pervaia polovina XIX veka* (Irkutsk: Irkutsk Technical University Press, 1996), 187.

5 Veniamin Bagrianskii, Bishop of Irkutsk 1789-1814, a monastic, educated at the Moscow Spiritual Academy and University of Leiden, Netherlands. See Naumova, op. cit., pp. 77–85 for additional information on this remarkable churchman.

:II: On Coming to Alaska

(IN ST. INNOCENT'S OWN WORDS)[1]

God's will for me was manifested foremost in my transfer from Irkutsk to Unalaska, that is, to America. I was consecrated deacon on 13 May 1817[2] and priest on 18 May 1821 in the same church where, as the author points out, I served until my departure for America. The visitor from Unalaska he mentions was, indeed, the apparent cause of my move to America. But it was not that his tales enchanted me personally. It was not so: in some aspects it happened as he says, in others differently.

This [American] visitor, a certain Ivan Kriukov, who had lived among the Aleuts for 40 years, stopped in our parish when he arrived in Irkutsk. He lived there from November almost to the middle of February. I was his spiritual advisor, as well as his entire family's, and therefore came to know him quite well. Yes, he told me very much, indeed, about America in general, and Aleuts in particular, and urged me by all possible means to go to Unalaska. But I was deaf to his stories and none of his arguments touched me.

To look at it realistically, from the human point of view, why should I go to God knows where when I was serving in one of the best parishes in the city, was respected by parishioners and even loved by them, under the eye of and in good standing with my superiors, had my own house, and income higher than the salary offered at Unalaska?

For these reasons, when by order of the late Archbishop Michael all priests in the diocese were being asked if they wished to go to Unalaska, and if they did not wish to do so, for what reasons, I was among those who signed stating that I did not wish to go to such a remote place. I wrote this in all sincerity, thinking that if our widows living only ten versts away from the authorities are left destitute (there was no charity organization to care for them at that time), what would happen ten thousand versts away? So I thought, and so I counseled my brethren.

But then, this same [American] visitor, who was urging me to go to Unalaska even as he bid me final farewell (I remember this vividly), on that same day, taking leave from the Archbishop (in whose living room I happened to be on this occasion for the first time), right then he began to speak about the Aleuts' zeal for prayer and for listening to the Word of God. I had doubtless heard this from him before and probably not only once. Then, and Glory to the Lord's Name!–suddenly, one may say, with my entire being–I became aflame with the desire to go to such people. I vividly remember even now my impatience waiting for the minute when I could declare my wish to the Archbishop. He was surprised, and said only: "we shall see."

How, in view of this, with any justice, can I take credit for that, or consider it a remarkable deed that I went to America? . . .

Notes

[1] In 1863 St. Innocent, then Archbishop Innokentii, responded in print to a biographical article written by his former seminary classmate, Archpriest [Protohierei] Gromov, correcting some inaccuracies. He was particularly concerned that his motivation for going to Alaska be presented correctly. We quote from the *Works of Innokentii, Metropolitan of Moscow*, collected by I. Barsukov, vol. 1, pp. 4-6 (See *Tvoreniia Innokentiia Mitropolita Moskovskogo* [Moscow: Synod Press, 1886]).

[2] All dates are in the Julian calendar. To convert them to the modern, Gregorian, calendar, add 12 days.

:III: Priest

St. Innocent sailed for Alaska on 30 August 1823 aboard the Russian-American Company sloop *Velikii Kniaz' Konstantin.* The voyage took almost two months–Sitka was sighted on 20 October. The navigation season was over and the family was obliged to spend the winter in Sitka.

The Church of St. Michael in Sitka, built in 1816, was served by the parish priest Aleksei Sokolov. St. Innocent assisted Fr. Sokolov, concelebrated the Divine services, and taught in the parish school. The clergy were not missionaries, but served the members of the Orthodox parish: Russian, Creole, Aleut, Alutiiq and a few Dena'ina employees of the Russian-American Company stationed at Sitka and the crews of the company and naval vessels which called at the port. In his spare time, St. Innocent studied the Aleut (Unangam) language, preparing himself for service in his assigned parish–the Unalaska district of the Russian-American Company. He also read voraciously, borrowing books from the Novoarkhangel'sk library and from friends he made in Sitka: young Semeon Ivanovich Ianovskii, departing the colonies with his bride, Irina Baranov; Kiril Khlebnikov, the manager of the Russian-American Company's head office in Alaska; and Capt. Matvei Ivanovich Murav'iev, the naval chief manager of the Russian establishment in Alaska 1820-1825.

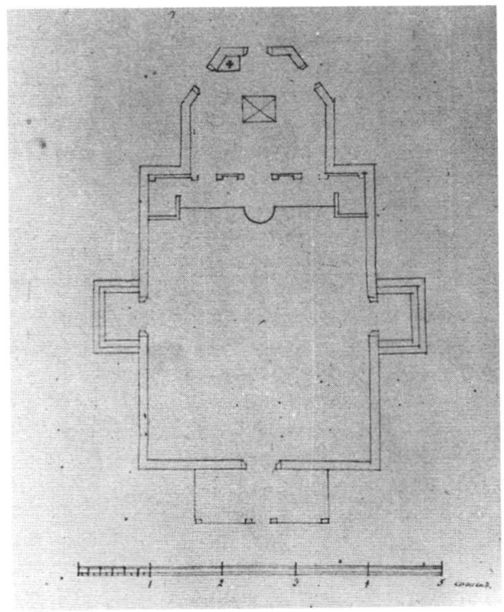

Plan of the Unalaska Church of the Holy Ascension of Christ submitted by St. Innocent for approval to Archbishop Michael of Irkutsk and Nerchinsk. Original in the Archives of St. Herman's Theological Seminary, Kodiak. Photo by L. Black, 1975.

After almost eight months in Sitka, the family sailed for Unalaska on 1 July 1825. By 29 July they reached their destination. The community welcomed them wholeheartedly. Eagerly, the parishioners awaited the first liturgy to be celebrated in their chapel, built in 1807/1808 under the leadership of since departed Fedor Burenin. On 1 August, St. Innocent celebrated his first Divine Liturgy in the Aleutians. On that day, the

Right: One of only two known representations of the church St. Innocent built in Unalaska 1825–1828. From a sketch by the Russian scholar I.G. Voznesenskii done in 1843. Originals are in the Archives of the Academy of Sciences of Russia, St. Petersburg.

Below: Two of the five icons painted by Vasilii Kriukov in 1828 for the iconostasy of St. Innocent's Church of the Holy Ascension of Christ in Unalaska.

Photos courtesy of the U.S. National Park Service.

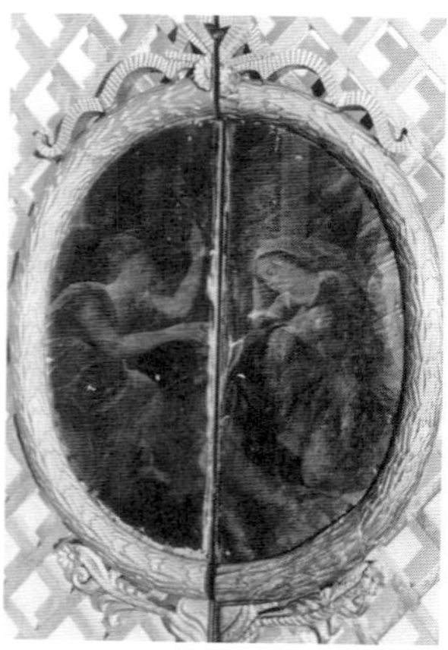

parishioners officially welcomed their first resident priest by presenting him with a formal written address and a gift of money to help him establish his household in the community.

The people also looked forward to a new church. St. Innocent was authorized to consecrate the church he was to build by a charter issued to him on 12 April 1823 by Michael, Archbishop of Irkutsk, and carried two antimins–a permanent one for the altar of the Church of the Holy Ascension of Christ in Unalaska, and the second to be used when traveling through the far-flung parish.[1]

St. Innocent drew a plan of the proposed new church. It was approved by Archbishop Michael and on 2 July 1825 the cornerstone was laid. A cross was raised at the spot. The three vessels in the harbor fired salutes. St. Innocent was the first to swing an axe. He worked on the construction, alongside his parishioners, until the church was completed.

In the meantime, services were held in the old chapel. On the Monday following the last service in the chapel (25 April 1825), the chapel was dismantled and the altar table and the iconostasy moved into the new church building. Only in 1828 was a new iconostasy completed, with icons painted by Vasilii Kriukov. Part of this iconostasy survives and forms the Royal Gates of the chapel of St. Sergius of Radonezh in the Unalaska church.[2]

St. Innocent traveled frequently to all the Aleut villages in the Unalaska district, visiting Nikolskoe on Umnak Island in the west, and Alaska Peninsula and Shumagin Islands settlements in the east. Most often he traveled by kayak or an open oar-propelled skin boat, the baidara. St. Innocent knew that many laymen either constructed small chapels on their own or had house chapels where they conducted services on a regular basis. He wanted to see proper chapels and prayer houses built in all the villages, but at that time the diocesan authorities refused to permit their establishment. To his great regret, even a request to build a new chapel at Nikolskoe, to replace the old one established in 1806 or even earlier by the Aleut *toion* Ivan Stepanovich Glotov, was rejected.[3]

His second, but no less important, goal was establishment of a school in accordance with his own educational philosophy. This he accomplished in a few years against many odds: books ordered for the school either failed to arrive or arrived late; there was a shortage of paper so that students practiced writing on the beach sand; in winter, there was a shortage of fuel, and teachers and students endured cold and damp; a new school building was badly needed. But St. Innocent persisted. He developed a new curriculum, encouraged enrollments, and maintained bilingual instruction. His brother Stephan, a sub-deacon in the Church, taught at the school also. He excelled as a mathematics teacher. A boarding school for girls from poor families was opened.

In order to follow successfully the bilingual mode of instruction, St. Innocent began to translate into Aleut as well as create instructional materials and spiritual literature in the Aleut language. In this task he was assisted by literate bilingual Aleuts, often of high standing in the Aleut community, such as the *toion* of the Krenitzin Islands, Ivan Pan'kov. The young priest and the much older Aleut leader became friends, as well as collaborators in the task of creating Aleut literacy. St. Innocent took every opportunity to visit Pan'kov in his home islands: Tigalda, Akun, Avatanok. On one of these trips, he encountered an Aleut healer and prophet, Ivan Smirennikov of Akun. It was said in the islands that Smirennikov had foretold St. Innocent's coming. A firm believer in the revelation of Divine truth to those chosen, St. Innocent told his people not to call Smirennikov a shaman, but a man of God.[4]

When the Russian-American Company offered transport on company vessels, St. Innocent visited the settlements of St. Paul and St. George, the Pribilof Islands. In 1829, he visited the Bristol Bay area and for the first time encountered the Yup'ik people of the Lower Nushagak. Kiril Khlebnikov was urging him to undertake missionary work among Alaska Natives who were not yet Christians, but St. Innocent did not see himself in that role. He was content to serve as parish priest among his devout Christian flock and dreamt of returning home. He did not want to remain in Alaska beyond 1831.

He devoted much time to education of his children,[5] to Aleut language studies, to collection of ethnographic and folkloric data, which he sent on to Kiril Khlebnikov in Sitka, and to the study of the Aleutian Archipelago environment.[6] High points interrupting the routine flow of life were the visits of various vessels, especially the vessels *Moller* and *Seniavin*, under the command of Captains Staniukovich and Litke, in 1828. A lifelong friendship with Litke was established.

Finally, in 1834, St. Innocent's request to be relieved of his post at Unalaska was granted, but the request to return home was not. He was, instead, transferred to Sitka.

Reproduction of a pencil sketch by an unknown artist, 1830s, of the Novoarkhangel'sk (Sitka) Church of St. Michael, where St. Innocent served as parish priest 1834-1838.

After published version in *Russkaia Amerika v zapiskakh Kirila Khlebnikova: Novoarkhangel'sk,* compiled, edited, and annotated by Svetlana G. Fedorova (Moscow: Nauka, 1985). Used by permission.

Sitka (1834–1838)

During Ferdinand P. Wrangell's tenure as Russian-American Company manager in Alaska (1830-1835), several changes affecting the Church took place. On Wrangell's request, the priest serving the Kodiak parish, Frumentii Mordovskii, was returned to Russia. The diocese was confronted with the need to replace him and their choice fell on the energetic and successful St. Innocent. Wrangell, however, wanted St. Innocent, whom he valued greatly, in Sitka. Fr. Sokolov took over the Kodiak parish and St. Innocent became the parish priest of Novoarkhangel'sk.

The four years he spent there were, like his years at Unalaska, very full. First, he began to lay the groundwork for construction of a new church to replace the old, dilapidated one. Secondly, he obtained the opportunity to interact more intensively with the Tlingit. Conversion of the Tlingit to Christianity began to occupy his thoughts. He tried to visit other *kwans*–local Tlingit communities–besides the Sitkan and used the opportunity, in October of 1837, to travel the Inside Passage as far south as the Stikine River and even Haida territory. His stay in Sitka, and his work with the Tlingit, was marred, however, by the smallpox outbreak which devastated the native population. "That horrible and unwanted guest," St. Innocent called the epidemic.

As the parish priest of Novoarkhangel'sk, he was responsible for the Settlement of Ross in California. In 1836, he traveled aboard the company vessel *Sitkha* to visit Ross and perform all the necessary services for the local population. He met the Indians living in the vicinity (largely the Pomo). He also visited the Catholic Missions of San Jose, San Rafael, Santa Clara, and San Francisco de Asis (Dolores) in San Francisco Bay. For the first time in his life he attended Catholic liturgy, witnessed a baptism and a funeral, and visited with several Catholic priests. They conversed in Latin.

In 1835, while in Sitka, St. Innocent was awarded the Order of St. Anna, 3d degree, in recognition of his service at Unalaska–an award for which the Archbishop of Irkutsk had recommended him in 1833.

By 1838 the diocesan authorities had finally relented and permitted St. Innocent to return to Russia. He sent his family via Okhotsk to Irkutsk, but he himself traveled on a circumnavigating naval vessel to St. Petersburg. He intended to supervise the publication of books in the Aleut language, and looked forward to the publication of his major ecological and ethnographic work *Notes on the Islands of the Unalashka District.*[7] In November of 1838 he left Sitka aboard the ship *Imperator Nikolai I*, Capt. Berens commanding.

Two of the Catholic missions St. Innocent visited in 1836: Santa Clara, top; San Francisco de Asis (Dolores), bottom.

Reproductions of paintings by Chesley Bonestell, courtesy Space Art International.

St. Petersburg and Moscow (1839-1841)

St. Innocent arrived in St. Petersburg on 25 June 1839. Here his time was spent in reporting to ecclesiastical authorities, meeting with Count Protasov, Ober-Procurator (President) of the Holy Ruling Synod, and arranging for publication of literature in the Aleut language. Through his old Alaskan friends, such as F.P. Litke and K. Khlebnikov, he was introduced to many influential persons and intellectuals. His first scholarly publications appeared in various journals as early as 1839, and several major publications followed in 1840-1846.

His report on *Condition of the Church in Russian settlements in America, with recommendations for their improvement* . . . was well received by the Synod and was recommended for publication. St. Innocent was elevated to the rank of archpriest, the highest office that could be held by a married ("white") clergyman, and in 1840 was awarded the Order of St. Anna, 2d and 1st degrees. The ecclesiastical authorities intended to send St.

Innocent back to Alaska, this time as dean of clergy with the mandate to reform and reorganize the churches there. St. Innocent agreed and began preparations for return to Alaska.

In the meantime, he traveled to Moscow, where he met and impressed Filaret, Metropolitan of Moscow and Kolomna, one of the most noted Russian Orthodox theologians of the time. He also made a pilgrimage to the Holy Trinity Monastery of St. Sergius of Radonezh.[8] Early in 1840, however, St. Innocent received news that his wife and his youngest son had died in Irkutsk. Concerned for the well-being of his orphaned children, he immediately petitioned the authorities for permission to return to Irkutsk. Instead, Metropolitan Filaret began pressuring St. Innocent to take monastic vows, thus paving the way for joining the episcopate.[9] St. Innocent refused several times, saying that the care of his family precluded such a step. He hesitated, even after a pilgrimage to the city of Kiev, the cradle of Russian Orthodoxy, and discussion with theologians there, and a meeting with the Synod, at which he was urged to follow Filaret's advice. Filaret then made arrangements for the care and education of St. Innocent's children. A renowned and influential noble, Aleksandr M. Potemkin, was appointed as their guardian and the imperial family became involved. Finally, St. Innocent bowed before the pressure and on 24 November 1840, the name day of his late wife Catherine, he submitted the petition for permission to become a monk. He was tonsured at the Holy Trinity Monastery of St. Sergius, taking the name of Innocent after St. Innocent of Irkutsk. The next day he was elevated to the rank of archimandrite.

Upon the urging of Emperor Nicholas I, the new Diocese of Kamchatka, the Kurile and Aleutian Islands was created by the Synod on 30 November 1840. The emperor also urged that St. Innocent be the first bishop of the new diocese. When the new Archimandrite Innokentii arrived in St. Petersburg, he was invited to the Winter Palace, where he celebrated services, met the emperor and the imperial family, and became a frequent guest, often teaching the imperial children about Alaska.

On 15 December 1840, Archimandrite Innokentii was consecrated bishop in the Cathedral of the Theotokos of Kazan' in St. Petersburg and appointed to serve the new diocese. Within a month, St. Innocent was on his way to Alaska to assume his new duties.

Cathedral of the Theotokos of Kazan', St. Petersburg, Russia, in the late 1820s. St. Innocent was consecrated bishop here on 15 December 1840.

Notes

1 An antimins is the icon that transforms a table into an altar. Divine Liturgy cannot be celebrated without an antimins (antimion). The antimion St. Innocent brought with him from Irkutsk to Unalaska survives. A photograph of it is featured in the exhibit.

2 A new church building was constructed during the tenure of Fr. Innokentii Shaiashnikov. Begun in 1853, the building was completed in 1858. The present church building was begun in 1894. In 1996, after major renovations, the church was reconsecrated by Metropolitan Theodosius of All America and Canada, with Bishop Vicar of Anchorage, Innocent, and Bishop of Yakutia German concelebrating. At that time a new antimins was placed on the altar.

3 Beginning in 1842, after St. Innocent returned to Alaska as bishop, many chapels were built in Alaska. Many of these chapels have now become churches.

4 St. Innocent's encounter with Smirennikov is represented in an icon put at our disposal by the Brotherhood of St. Innocent in Moscow and in a secular print by American artist Ray Hudson of Middlebury, Vermont, formerly of Unalaska, "Shaman Smirennikov foretells the coming of Veniaminov."

5 See the essay "A Very Human Story," this volume. St. Innocent had seven children who survived infancy, five of them born in Unalaska.

6 See the essay "Scholar," this volume.

7 Published in Russian in 1840 as *Zapiski ob ostrovakh Unalashkinskago otdela* (St. Petersburg: Russian-American Company), and in English translation in 1984 (Kingston, Ontario, Canada: The Limestone Press).

8 Known as *Sergiev Posad* (St. Sergius' plantation), but during Soviet times referred to as Zagorsk.

9 In the Orthodox Churches, only unmarried (single or widowed) clergymen could become bishops.

St. Innocent as bishop, 1840, from a portrait now lost. Original photo in the State Museum of History and Culture of the Peoples of the North, Republic of Sakha (Yakutia), Yakutsk, Russian Federation.

Courtesy of the Museum and the State Archive of the Sakha Republic.

:IV: Bishop, 1840–1850

St. Innocent lost no time in commencing the arduous trip overland across Russia and then by ship from Okhotsk to Novoarkhangel'sk (Sitka). He did stop on the way in Irkutsk, where he, now a bishop, celebrated the Divine Service in the city's main cathedral and then in the Church of the Annunciation, where he first served as deacon. He also visited the seminary and thanked his old teachers. He visited the cemetery and celebrated the service for the dead for his wife and other kin.[1] Then he traveled to Anga, where his children were, and dispatched them to St. Petersburg to enter various educational institutions. The two surviving boys, Innokentii and Gavriil, entered the St. Petersburg Seminary. The girls, with the exception of the eldest, Catherine, were admitted to various boarding schools for girls. Catherine was married in Irkutsk to a young clergyman, Il'ia Petelin, and she and her husband accompanied St. Innocent to Alaska.

St. Innocent and his suite sailed aboard the *Okhotsk* and went ashore at Sitka on 29 September 1841. His suite consisted of Hieromonk Misail, dean of clergy and later an able missionary to the Tlingit; Hierodeacon Nikolai, later hieromonk, first missionary at Kenai; Deacon Serapion Mamin; Deacon Il'ia Petelin; Hypo-deacon Lev Popov; seminarian Il'ia Tyzhnov; seminarian Mikhailo Masiukov, who served as choir director; and choristers Andrei Blagovidov, Petr Berdennikov, Prokopii Letvintsov and Konstantin Zarudenkov.

Within days, St. Innocent was busy creating the administrative structure for the diocese; the diocesan consistory was opened on 14 October 1841. He proved to be an outstanding administrator. There were clear lines of communication and excellent record keeping both at the chancery and in the parishes. Today, these records provide priceless information on the history of Alaskan peoples and of the Orthodox Church in Alaska.

St. Innocent's next priority was the establishment of an ecclesiastical school in order to prepare clergy to serve his enormous diocese. By December, such a school was already functioning. By 1845, it was consolidated with the ecclesiastical school of Petropavlovsk-Kamchatskii and reorganized as a seminary. For years, this institution produced a number of outstanding graduates who served Alaska faithfully and well, one generation after another. With the enthusiastic support of the chief manager of the Russian-American Company in Alaska, A. Etolin (Etholen), a special building was constructed to serve as bishop's residence and to house the school and consistory administrative offices. Today, this building is a museum, maintained by the U.S. National Park Service.

"I am well and live in the bishop's house, of two stories, and have a house church consecrated 15 December 1843. The iconostasy is of local workmanship, with icons which came around the world in 1841 from Her Excellency [Countess] A.A. Orlov."

Letter to Andrei N. Murav'iev 2/14 April 1844, Novoarkhangel'sk.

As bishop, St. Innocent had the responsibility of introducing the Christian faith to Native peoples of Alaska who as yet were not within the orbit of the Church. The Yup'ik people, who inhabit the area from Bristol Bay to Seward Peninsula, were his first concern, for many had been converted to Orthodoxy by laymen, as St. Innocent had learned on his visit there as a priest of Unalaska parish. The Nushagak Mission was created by the end of 1841. His son-in-law, Il'ia Petelin, now a priest, was assigned to serve this mission. He was assisted by Deacon Vasilii D. Shishkin, an able and dedicated man. Two other missions were established in 1844–1845. One was at Ikogmiut on the Yukon to serve the Yup'ik, Inupiaq and Athabaskan peoples from Unalakleet and St. Michael to the Innoko and Kuskokwim River basins under Fr. Iakov Netsvetov, St. Innocent's old coworker from Atka. The other was at Kenai, where Hieromonk Nikolai served the Chugach, the Upper Alaska Peninsula Alutiiq, and Athabaskan peoples (Dena'ina and Ahtna) until his death. Churches were built in all of these communities soon after the establishment of the missions. A mission to the eastern and inland Tlingit, along the Stikine River, was projected.

Left: Holy Gospel printed in 1746, given to St. Innocent in 1840 by St. Sergius Holy Trinity Monastery.

Right: St. Innocent's miter.

At each mission, and in many villages where relatively well educated lay readers performed services, St. Innocent encouraged establishment of schools. By 1849, no fewer than fourteen schools functioned in rural Alaska, even in such remote places as Attu and Amlia.

Under St. Innocent's episcopal authority, villages were now permitted to built chapels where laymen conducted services.

One of the first such chapels was built on Akun, by St. Innocent's old friend Ivan Pan'kov and comrades. Most of the Orthodox village churches in Alaska have their origins in these chapels built and consecrated during St. Innocent's tenure as bishop.

St. Innocent felt it absolutely necessary to visit remote areas of his diocese personally, and for this reason undertook extremely arduous journeys. In the spring of 1842 he visited Kodiak and celebrated the service for the dead at the grave of St. Herman of Alaska on Spruce Island. That same year he commenced his first inspection tour through the diocese. He visited Unga, Unalaska, St. Paul and St. George, Atka (where he collected Fr. Iakov Netsvetov and asked that he accompany his bishop), the Commandor Islands, and thence to Petropavlovsk-Kamchatskii. He wintered in Kamchatka, visiting remote villages by dog- and reindeer sled. He renewed his acquaintance with a classmate from Irkutsk Seminary, Fr. Prokopii Gromov, who was serving in Petropavlovsk, and visited his brother, Fr. Stephan Veniaminov, in Lesnoi on Gizhiga Bay in northern Kamchatka. He traveled to Okhotsk overland by dog sled, returning to Sitka by Russian-American Company ship in September 1843.

The second tour, which once again took him to Kamchatka, began in the fall of 1844 and ended in the fall of 1845; the third

A view of the Tlingit Church of the Holy Resurrection (also designated in literature as the Church of the Holy Trinity).

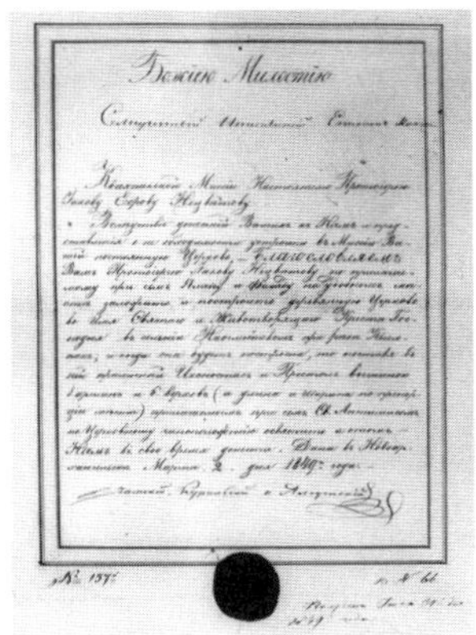

Above: The charter issued in 1849 by St. Innocent to Fr. Iakov Netsvetov to build the Church of the Elevation of the Holy Cross at Ikogmiut (now Russian Mission).

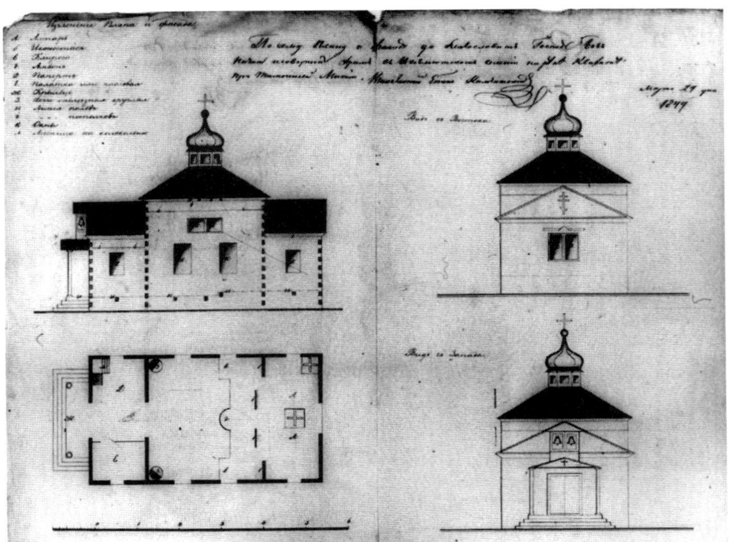

Left: Plan for the church at Ikogmiut by Fr. Iakov Netsvetov (now St. Iakov, Enlightener of Alaska Native Peoples).

occurred in 1846–1847. In 1848, St. Innocent traveled from Sitka to the Eastern Aleutians and the Pribilof Islands, then northward to St. Michael. There he met Fr. Iakov Netsvetov and his assistants, Konstantin Lukin of Kolmakovskii Redoubt on the Kuskokwim and Innokentii Shaiashnikov of Unalaska who served with Fr. Iakov at Ikogmiut Mission. St. Innocent consecrated the young Innokentii Shaiashnikov priest at St. Michael and brought him to Unalaska to serve as priest of his home parish until his death in 1883. From Unalaska, he traveled once again to Kodiak. A fourth tour, by now a regular occurrence, took place in 1849.

In this, his last year as bishop, St. Innocent consecrated the Tlingit Church of the Holy Resurrection[2] in Sitka, where services were held in the Tlingit language. Plans for the Church of the Elevation of the Holy Cross at Ikogmiut were approved, as was the plan for the new Cathedral of St. Michael at Novoarkhangel'sk (Sitka). The construction of this cathedral commenced in 1850. New missions in Kamchatka, along the Okhotsk Sea littoral, in Chukotka, and at Anadyr' in eastern Siberia were established.

In the fall, St. Innocent once again set out on an inspection tour of his diocese, sailing from Sitka to the recently established port of Aian on the Okhotsk Sea. It was there that he learned that on 21 April 1850 the Synod had elevated him to the status of archbishop and that his diocese had been enlarged to include Yakutia.[3]

Notes

1 St. Innocent visited the graves of his wife and other kin buried in Irkutsk whenever he visited the city. His wife's grave was marked by a stone monument. The cemetery was converted into a park of "Culture and Rest" during the Soviet period and all markers obliterated.

2 In some documents referred to as Holy Trinity church.

3 Previously, Yakutia was part of the Irkutsk Diocese.

:V: Archbishop, 1850–1867

As archbishop, St. Innocent had to face expanded, and heavier, responsibilities as well as a rapidly changing demographic and political situation in the Asiatic part of his archdiocese. The population of the diocese, stretching from the Arctic Ocean to the Amur River valley and maritime regions in the south, numbered in the millions, some inhabiting ancient Russian cities, others scattered in remote, small settlements, and a large proportion leading a nomadic life as reindeer herders, and hunter/foragers. Among the Russian settlers of the area were many Old Believers who had fled into the wilderness of eastern Siberia after the reform of the Church instituted in the reign of Tsar Alexis and the persecution that followed, especially under Peter the Great.[1] There were also members of strange small sects such as *khlysty*.[2] The ethnographic fabric was even more complex: from the northern Ainu of the Kurile Islands, to the Itel'men (Kamchadal) and Koriak of Kamchatka, the Chukchi of the Chukotka Peninsula, the Even and Evenk of the Siberian taiga, the Yukagir in the extreme north of Yakutia and, of course, the numerous Yakut. Some Buriat settlements were also within his jurisdiction and in the south, Mongolians, Manchu, Chinese, and Koreans were encountered. This was a world of many tongues, and of diverse ways of life, from agriculturalists and cattle breeders to reindeer herders, fishermen, whalers and hunters.

Blagoveshchensk, at the confluence of the Amur and Zeia Rivers, founded by St. Innocent when he established the Cathedral of the Annunciation and transferred his see to this location.

Engraving from *Zhivopisnaia Rossiia* v.12, part 2 (St. Petersburg/Moscow: M.O. Volf, 1895).

St. Innocent drew on his Alaskan experience and, especially in the beginning of his new service, transferred his old and proven Alaskan colleagues to the Asiatic mainland to facilitate work among his new flock. Among these were his son-in-law Il'ia Petelin, appointed to Nel'kan near the Port of Aian in the Even region, and, in 1853, his son Gavriil (who had served for a few years in Alaska where he was born), assigned to the Lower

Amur River area. Fr. Gavriil Veniaminov was the first Orthodox priest to set foot on the Island of Sakhalin.

As mentioned elsewhere, in 1850 St. Innocent was on a tour of his diocese, traveling, as always, by dog- and reindeer team. Upon returning to Aian, and learning of the changes in his duties, he traveled, in 1852, to Yakutsk for the first time in his official capacity as archbishop. In addition, St. Innocent had been appointed the *hegumen* (abbot) of the oldest eastern Siberian monastery, that of the Savior in Yakutsk. Then he returned to Sitka, overland as far as Aian and thence by ship. This was his last visit to Alaska. In 1853 he took up residence in Yakutsk as abbot of the Savior Monastery. In 1858, his see was officially transferred to Yakutsk, as was the seminary. While in Yakutia, he initiated a massive long-term effort to translate church literature into the indigenous languages, primarily into Yakut. In 1859, he celebrated the Liturgy in Yakutsk in the Yakut language. But, while carrying out his duties as archpastor of an enormous diocese, St. Innocent became more and more involved in the affairs of state due to circumstances beyond his control.

The so-called Crimean War, between Russia on one side and Turkey, France and Britain on the other, was fought in 1854–1855. At that time, the two European powers sought to expand their influence in the North Pacific basin. With China, Russia's neighbor along the Amur River, greatly weakened in the wake of the Opium Wars, and conditions of war obtaining, it was deemed a good time to attempt to seize Russia's Pacific littoral. Combined British and French naval forces attacked along the front stretching from Sakhalin and the Kurile Islands to Petropavlovsk-Kamchatskii.[3] Repulsed at Petropavlovsk, they followed a hit-and-run policy in several areas, seizing prisoners, often civilians, even clergy. In the summer of 1855, the British came to Aian at the same time as St. Innocent was visiting that port, which had been deserted by the majority of the inhabitants. The British entered the church while St. Innocent was celebrating the services there and were about to take him prisoner. St. Innocent, who had met a number of British naval officers in Sitka, not only managed to persuade them to let him be, but also effected the release of a priest and civilians who had been seized elsewhere. Afterwards, he entertained the British officers at the parish house. It is possible that it was St.

Innocent's presence which deterred the British from destroying the Aian settlement.

Port of Aian, where in 1855 St. Innocent encountered invading British naval forces.

St. Innocent worked closely with the Russian naval personnel, and specifically with Governor-General Murav'iev-Amurskii, consolidating Russia's hold on the region. St. Innocent wrote an important position paper describing the ecological conditions of the area and outlining its economic potential. He also wrote a paper on the importance and future development of eastern Siberian trade. His visits to the Amur and Maritime regions of the Russian Far East became frequent. St. Innocent advocated, and then participated in, the founding of many new settlements, now important cities and industrial centers: Nikolaevsk-on-Amur, Khabarovsk, Mariinsk, Vladivostok, and finally Blagoveshchensk.[4]

He participated in several river journeys along the Amur, accompanying Murav'iev-Amurskii. In 1856, he met the Chinese diplomats and then again, in 1858, was present at the signing of the Treaty of Aigun, which established the border between China and Russia. On 9 May 1858, St. Innocent celebrated the Liturgy and laid the foundation stone of the Cathedral of the Annunciation at a locality near the confluence of the rivers Zeia and Amur, thus founding the City of Blagoveshchensk. In 1862, he transferred his see from Yakutsk to Blagoveshchensk, where he hoped to end his service and enjoy growing fruit trees. The river fascinated him and later, when settled at Blagoveshchensk, he often traveled along it navigating his own motor craft. But other journeys were yet to come.

Below: Chinese settlement of Aigun, where the Treaty of Aigun determining the Russo-Chinese border was signed. St. Innocent witnessed the signing.

Bottom: Nikolaevsk-on-Amur.

Engravings from *Zhivopisnaia Rossiia* v.12, part 2 (St. Petersburg/ Moscow: M.O. Volf, 1895).

All the same, he never neglected his duties as a churchman. From the 1850s on, he was required to attend from time to time the meetings of the Synod, the ruling body of the Orthodox Church. In August of 1856, while on one such visit to the capital cities, St. Innocent attended the coronation of Tsar Alexander II. However, this obligatory attendance added to his travels and took up much of his time. He began to petition for the appointment of bishop vicars, one for Alaska, one for Yakutia. On 29 March 1859

Right: The Old Cathedral of the Epiphany in Irkutsk. Here, St. Innocent participated in services from 1841 to 1867, and consecrated Bishops Petr and Pavel.

From a postcard by an unknown photographer, reproduced by Vladimir Gul'iaev, courtesy of Oleg V. Bychkov, Irkutsk.

Petr (Peter), Bishop Vicar of Novoarkhangel'sk (Sitka) 1859–1867.

Photo courtesy of the State Library of the Republic of Sakha (Yakutia), Russian Federation.

Pavel (Paul), Bishop Vicar of Yakutia, 1860–1867, Bishop Vicar of Novoarkhangel'sk 1867–1868.

Photo courtesy of the State Library of the Republic of Sakha (Yakutia), Russian Federation.

he consecrated as bishop Archimandrite Petr, formerly dean of the Novoarkhangel'sk seminary, and appointed him Vicar to Alaska.[5] In 1860, St. Innocent consecrated as his Bishop Vicar for Yakutia widowed priest Petr Popov, who took the name Pavel.[6]

Hoping to travel perhaps for the last time to Alaska, he went in 1861 to Nikolaevsk-on-Amur. Having suffered shipwreck, he visited instead various places in the Maritime Region, from Khabarovsk to Vladivostok, as transportation was offered, and then sailed to Hakodate in Japan, where he concelebrated services with Nicholas, now St. Nicholas of Japan, and urged him to learn–and teach in–the Japanese language. That fall he visited Kamchatka for the last time. The next year, 1862, his services were recognized with the award of the Order of St. Alexander Nevskii.

In 1865 he visited Yakutsk for the last time. He also began laying the groundwork for establishment of Yakutia as a separate diocese. Appointed permanent member of the Ruling Synod, St. Innocent officially raised in the next year (1866) the question of his retirement–perhaps in St. Petersburg, even though he was not all that fond of the city. He likened it to a blacksmith shop: the choice was being burned or getting dirty.

In 1867 St. Innocent was awarded the Order of St. Vladimir. But this was not a lucky year. His beloved Alaska was sold to the United States. Eyesight failing, and feeling his age, St. Innocent longed for peace. He did not know that on 26 November his friend, mentor, and patron, the Metropolitan of Moscow, had died and that he would be called to take his place.

Notes

1 St. Innocent sought a way to reconcile with the Old Believers and attempted to effect such a reconciliation with certain segments of this population.

2 Members of this sect, both male and female, practiced self-castration.

3 Alaska, by an agreement engineered by the Hudson's Bay Company and the Russian-American Company, was declared neutral territory, but St. Innocent spent many a worrying hour believing that the French would refuse to observe Alaska's neutrality. Russian-American Company ships were seized at sea by the British.

4 *Nechto ob Amure.*

5 Petr (Peter) was not St. Innocent's first choice. He did prove not fully satisfactory and was replaced in Alaska in 1867. In an uncharacteristically open criticism in a letter to personal friend Dimitrii Khitrov, in which Petr's transfer to a remote monastery is discussed, St. Innocent wrote that "maybe there, finally, he [Petr] will learn that humans are not and cannot be angels."

6 In 1867 Bishop Pavel (Paul) replaced Petr as Bishop Vicar in Alaska.

:VI: Metropolitan, 1868–1879

Upon receiving notification that he was to assume the highest office of the Russian Orthodox Church, before leaving Blagoveshchensk for Moscow, the ancient Russian capital,[1] St. Innocent consecrated as the first independent Bishop of Yakutia his old friend, Dimitrii Khitrov (monastic name: Dionisii). The ceremony was conducted in the new Blagoveshchensk Cathedral of the Annunciation on 7 February 1868. A week later, on 15 February, St. Innocent left Blagoveshchensk forever. He traveled slowly, stopping along the way in many cities and towns to celebrate a service for the faithful, who met him with the bells of all churches ringing.

Metropolitan Innocent.

The stop in Irkutsk in March of that year was the most meaningful for St. Innocent personally. As the head of the Russian Orthodox Church, he celebrated the first service in that city in its cathedral, but the next day he offered Divine Liturgy in the Church of the Annunciation where he had begun his service as deacon in 1817. Then he visited the seminary and celebrated the Divine Service there. Paschal services were held in the cathedral and, after a visit to the cemetery, St. Innocent went–for the last time in his life–to his home in Anga.

As mentioned elsewhere, throughout his career St. Innocent fostered education and the establishment of educational institutions. He also founded, and encouraged others to found, scholarships. While he was in Irkutsk, the commercial center of eastern Russia, merchants of that city established several scholarships in his honor, including one to Moscow University for a Siberian student.

In Kazan', St. Innocent received at the hands of Archbishop Antonii the sign of his new rank: the white bishop's headdress decorated with the diamond cross, worn only by the Metropolitan of Moscow. In Nizhnii Novgorod, St. Innocent boarded a train for Moscow.

Arriving on 25 May 1868, he was met by the leading clergy and immediately proceeded to the retreat at the Holy Trinity Monastery of St. Sergius of Radonezh. Only on the following day did he enter the main Moscow cathedral, that of the Dormition of the Theotokos in the Kremlin. On 31 May he returned to the Holy Trinity Monastery: as Metropolitan of Moscow and Kolomna he was the hegumen (abbot) of that monastery. This holy place, where he was tonsured a monk in 1840, was to be his home to the end of his days.

Nevertheless, his life was not one of a recluse, nor of contemplation. His responsibilities were many. Innovation and reform were in his plans. One of the first measures he instituted was the improvement of the material lives of village clergy. He also officially permitted the ordination of single men as priests without requiring them to become monks (a practice he had followed in his diocese as archbishop). He actively encouraged the formation of Benevolent Societies to care for destitute old clergy and the widows and orphans of deceased ones, and created a committee for the establishment of homes for ailing and destitute clergy and their families. He saw the benefits of the monastic tradition in religious life and argued against those who proposed monastery closures. Indeed, he reorganized administration of the monasteries.

Foremost, he did everything he could to ensure that Orthodox clergy in Alaska, now under United States sovereignty, received material support. He redefined the Orthodox mission in America: with the ever-growing influx of Orthodox immigrants from Eastern Europe to the United States and Canada, the Church had to serve a much wider community than the Orthodox Alaskans. He believed that the now independent American Diocese should consider establishing its administrative center in one of the major urban centers in the United States, either New York or San Francisco. The use of English in Divine services and in parish schools and seminaries was to be fostered to enable the Americans and Canadians to come to know, and be attracted to, the Church.

In 1869 he revitalized a moribund missionary society. This new missionary society was not aimed at foreign countries (with the exception of raising funds for Alaskan churches), but was to focus on introduction of Christianity among the non-Christian populations of the Russian Empire. St. Innocent was in contact with two Episcopal bishops in the United States He dreamt of an ecumenical world council. He had already entertained such an idea as archbishop: he wanted the schism to heal and heresies to disappear. He encouraged concelebration and participation in Orthodox Divine services by Armenian clergy and even by the Old Believers who sought reconciliation with Orthodoxy in some way. He planned to put his proposal for such a council before the sovereign.

In 1873 St. Innocent established in Moscow, in a house donated by Moscow merchant D.I. Khliudov, the School of Iconography, to which was attached a museum of iconography. St. Innocent defined the mission of this school as the provision of opportunities for talented children of the poor. Ten scholarships were established by Khliudov, urged on by St. Innocent. The school opened its doors on 30 September 1873 with a Te Deum celebrated by St. Innocent.

Educational reform and participation of the Church in universal education were much on his mind. He joined (if not formed) the Society for Spiritual Education; effected the opening of the Diocesan Spiritual School for Women in Moscow, named for the late Metropolitan Filaret; and became a patron of the Brotherhood of Mary Magdalene, Equal to the Apostles. The goal of this last-named society was creation of schools for both men and women. As always, St. Innocent made generous donations, giving 18,000 rubles for the Diocesan School for Women. He supported many causes and never forgot his roots: as metropolitan, he gave capital of 6,500 rubles to Anga village, the interest to be used for the maintenance of the Church of St. Elias where his father had been sacristan and his uncle a reader.

He also was extremely concerned about the Aleuts, learning in 1871 that they were suffering a serious economic plight and that social ills were becoming rampant.

His efforts were recognized by the Church and by the government. On 16 April 1872, St. Innocent was awarded the Order of St. Andrew the First Called, the highest award in Imperial Russia, established in the seventeenth century by Peter the Great. Earlier, in 1869, he was elected honorary member of the Imperial Geographic Society and honorary member of the faculty of Moscow University. Alphonse L. Pinart, the French scholar who studied Alaskan languages and ethnography in the early 1870s, met St. Innocent in St. Petersburg and later asked permission to dedicate a forthcoming book on Alaska Native ethnography to him.

Correspondence with Nicholas (St. Nicholas of Japan) and with his old seminary classmates and friends gave him much pleasure. His son Gavriil was with him in Moscow, providing personal support when he felt himself weakening. Working with the architect on construction of the metropolitan's summer residence, Cherkizovo, gave him the opportunity to indulge in his old love: architectural design.

He was delighted when Aleuts came to Moscow to visit in 1870. One of them, M. Berezkin, remained as his *keleinik* (personal attendant), returning to Alaska only after St. Innocent's death. Perhaps it was with this delegation that St. Innocent sent to the village chapel of Kashega, Unalaska Island, the icon of the Transfiguration which is today one of the treasures in the Cathedral of the Holy Ascension of Christ in Unalaska. That same year he sent an icon of the Holy Life-Creating Trinity to the City of Yakutsk as his blessing.

In 1877, Charles Reuben Hale, an American Episcopal clergyman, published the first biography of St. Innocent and called him an apostle. Hale's work is entitled *Innocent of Moscow, the Apostle of Kamchatka and Alaska.* In 1878, the Episcopal Bishop of Kentucky, Benjamin B. Smith, sent a copy to St. Innocent in Moscow.

By this time, St. Innocent was almost totally blind (a cataract operation in 1870 was unsuccessful). His health was failing and he foresaw the end. On the eve of the Paschal Feast in the spring of 1879, a long and active life dedicated to the people and the Church, the life of A Good and Faithful Servant, drew to a close.

Three views of Cherkizovo, the metropolitan's summer residence. Here St. Innocent indulged his passion for architecture for the last time, actively participating in the building's design and planning.

Photos provided courtesy of A.A. Istomin, RAN, Institute of Ethnography and Anthropology, Moscow.

Note

1 St. Petersburg was designated the imperial capital by Peter the Great, but Moscow remained the spiritual capital of Russia. The tsars were crowned in Moscow in the Cathederal of the Dormition (Uspenskii sobor) in the Kremlin.

УКАЗАНІЕ ПУТИ
ЦАРСТВІЕ НЕБЕСНОЕ.
ТИКИ АН-КА-У ХАН-ТЕ.
ЧАСТЬ ПЕРВАЯ.
ЮБИЛЕЙНОЕ ИЗДАНІЕ.
СИТХА.

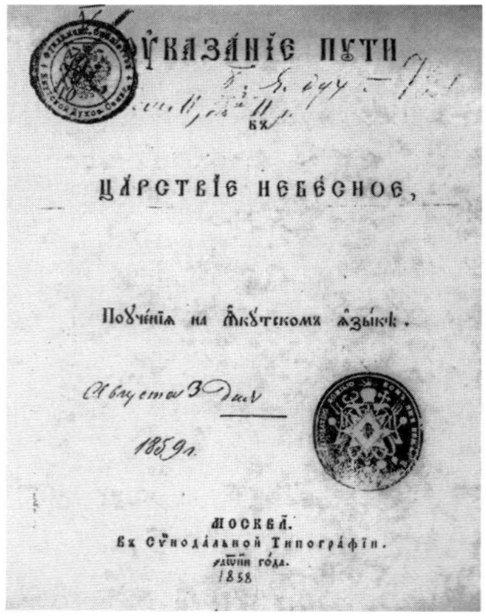

УКАЗАНІЕ ПУТИ
КЪ
ЦАРСТВІЕ НЕБЕСНОЕ,
Поученія на Якутскомъ языкѣ.
МОСКВА.
Въ Сѵнодальной Типографіи.
1858

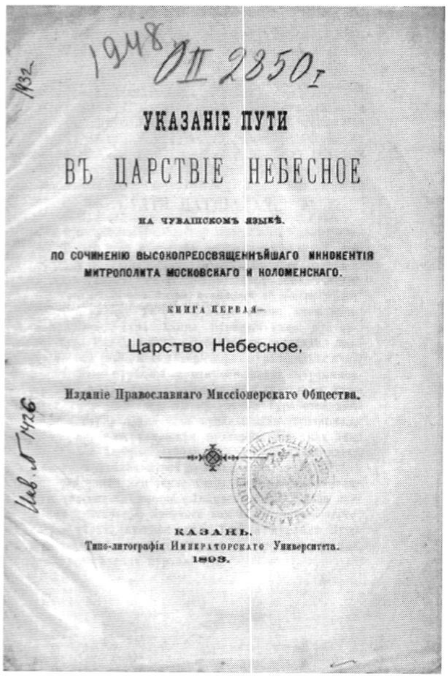

УКАЗАНІЕ ПУТИ
ВЪ ЦАРСТВІЕ НЕБЕСНОЕ
НА ЧУВАШСКОМЪ ЯЗЫКѢ.
ПО СОЧИНЕНІЮ ВЫСОКОПРЕОСВЯЩЕННѢЙШАГО ИННОКЕНТІЯ
МИТРОПОЛИТА МОСКОВСКАГО И КОЛОМЕНСКАГО.
КНИГА ПЕРВАЯ
Царство Небесное.
Изданіе Православнаго Миссіонерскаго Общества.
КАЗАНЬ.
Типо-литографія Императорскаго Университета.
1893.

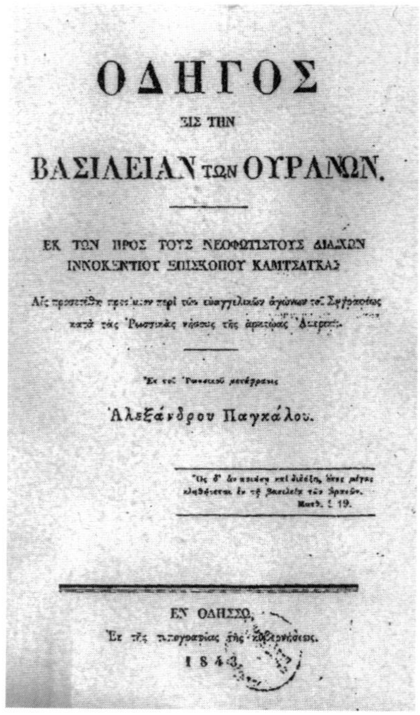

ΟΔΗΓΟΣ
ΕΙΣ ΤΗΝ
ΒΑΣΙΛΕΙΑΝ ΤΩΝ ΟΥΡΑΝΩΝ.
ΕΚ ΤΩΝ ΠΡΟΣ ΤΟΥΣ ΝΕΟΦΩΤΙΣΤΟΥΣ ΔΙΑΛΕΞΩΝ
ΙΝΝΟΚΕΝΤΙΟΥ ΕΠΙΣΚΟΠΟΥ ΚΑΜΤΣΑΤΚΑΣ
Ἀλεξάνδρου Παγκάλου.
ΕΝ ΟΔΗΣΣΩ,
1843.

Title pages from St. Innocent's 1833 book Indication of the Way to the Kingdom of Heaven, *originally written in Aleut, in the languages of (clockwise from top left) Tlingit, Yakut, Greek, and Chuvash.*

:VII: Theologian

Indication of the Way to the Kingdom of Heaven

St. Innocent was recognized early in his lifetime as a brilliant theologian. Well versed in Orthodox, particularly patristic, theological literature, he also voraciously read Western works, both Catholic and German Protestant, either in Russian translation or in Latin. He was tolerant of other faiths, but especially so of the faith of indigenous peoples of Alaska, Siberia, and the Russian Far East. In accordance with patristic tradition, he saw the Holy Spirit manifest itself among non-Christian peoples. He often expressed his feelings on the subject in letters to friends and colleagues.

He wrote about his admiration for the heroism and self-sacrifice of Tlingit warriors who voluntarily met death in order to prevent a blood feud between clans, likening their courage to that of early martyrs. He bowed before the faith of an Evenk he met in northern Kamchatka, and other peoples of eastern Siberia, citing in a letter to Norov, Procurator of the Synod, the words of an Evenk:

> A Tungus always prays. A Tungus knows that all is given by God. When I kill a partridge, I know that it was given me by God and I pray to God and offer thanks to Him; if I fail to take a partridge, this also is from God, who withheld the game from me; it means I was not good and therefore I also pray to God.

St. Innocent commented:

> I cannot remember these words without my heart being moved, especially since these words, truly Christian words, were spoken by a man whom our new philosophers would not dignify with the name of a human being. . . . And one thing more: the more I become acquainted with the savages, the more I am convinced that these so-called savages are much, much better in respect to ethics [moral life] than the so-called enlightened ones. It follows then: we, with our enlightenment, move away from, do not come closer to, perfection. And it must be so: we abandoned the source of the water of life and dig ourselves safe wells. . . . My flock is small in numbers (up to 18½ thousand) but not small, not in the least, in virtue. It is not only the Aleut, as I thought earlier, who know how or knew

> how to share the last fish with the hungry, not they alone who are patient [in adversity], modest, obedient, peaceful and pious, etc. All the small peoples (we cannot call them nations because of their small numbers) living within the borders of the Kamchatkan Diocese evidence the same qualities. Only in piety, devotion to the faith, and in attention to God's word do the Aleuts occupy the first place. Even Chukchi and Koriak who are not baptized have many good qualities and customs. Hospitality, self-respect and respect for one's name, honesty, keeping one's word, readiness to assist the hungry without any kind of expectation of recompense–all is a common custom of almost all local indigenous peoples. Among the unbaptized and independent ones there are traces of ancient customs. For example, unchastity is punished among the Koriak by death. . . . The more I come to know the so-called savages the more I love them and become ever more convinced that we, with all our enlightenment, left the way toward perfection, almost imperceptibly. . . . In the entire Kamchatkan Diocese there is no thievery or murder; at least there are no instances in which a Tungus, a Kamchadal, or an Aleut is in court for such crimes. On the contrary, there are many instances of virtue. . . . I cannot avoid saying, in the spirit of gratitude, blessed be the Lord who reveals knowledge of faith and truth to infants and conceals it from those who believe themselves to be the wise ones.[1]

As early as 1842, in letters to friends, St. Innocent expressed interest in the ecumenical activities of Dean Palmer from England and returned to this interest toward the end of his life, as metropolitan. He dreamt of a time when mankind would be united in one faith, without rancor or compulsion, and schisms would become things of the past.

Many of his addresses and sermons were published after his death in various journals and a selection appeared in the compendium of St. Innocent's works compiled and edited by I. Barsukov. Of these, the most important are *Thoughts and Remarks on Various Aspects of Church Life* (1868) and three articles on the community life in monasteries (1868, 1869, and 1896). One of the works of theological significance available in the English language is St.Innocent's *Instructions to a Priest Assigned to Convert Believers of Other Faith and for Guidance of those who Have Converted to Christianity.* Written in 1841, in the first year of his ministry as bishop, it has been republished several times and a later version, issued in the 1850s to Hieromonk Feofil, newly appointed to Nushagak Mission among the Yup'ik, was printed in parallel Russian and English texts in the *American Orthodox Messenger* in 1899.[2] Another work available in English is his *Condition of the Orthodox Church in Russian America* (1899, written in 1839 and published in Russian in 1840),[3] and *Condition of the Orthodox Church in Russian America* (1972).[4]

However, St. Innocent's most important theological work is his *Indication of the Way to the Kingdom of Heaven.* Written in Aleut in 1833, first published in Aleut in 1840, it has been translated into many languages: Russian, Old Church Slavonic, Greek, Arabic, Japanese, English, and many languages of the indigenous peoples of Russia and Alaska. It is used by Christians of many faiths today and is even available on the Internet. The most recent English edition is that of 1993, Holy Trinity Monastery, Jordanville, New York. The Aleut text in both old and new orthography, transliterated by Iliodor Philemonof of St. George, Alaska, has been produced this year (1997) by the Alaska Native Language Center, University of Alaska Fairbanks, with a scholarly introduction delineating the history of this work by Dr. Michael Krauss, the center's director.

Notes

1 See Barsukov, *Pis'ma* . . . (Letters . . .), vol.1, 1897:97, 102-103, 104-106.

2 See vol. 3, no. 20, pp. 534-543 for part I and no. 21, pp. 564-574 for part II.

3 An excerpt has been reprinted in *Orthodoxy and Native Americans: The Alaskan Mission*, by Barbara S. Smith (Crestwood, N.Y.: St. Vladimir Seminary Press, 1980).

4 Originally published in Russian, *Sostoianie Pravoslavnoi Tserkvi v Rossiiskoi Amerike* (St. Petersburg: Imperial Academy of Sciences, 1840). English translation, edited, with commentary by Robert Nichols and Robert Croskey, *Pacific Northwest Quarterly*, 1972, 2:41-54.

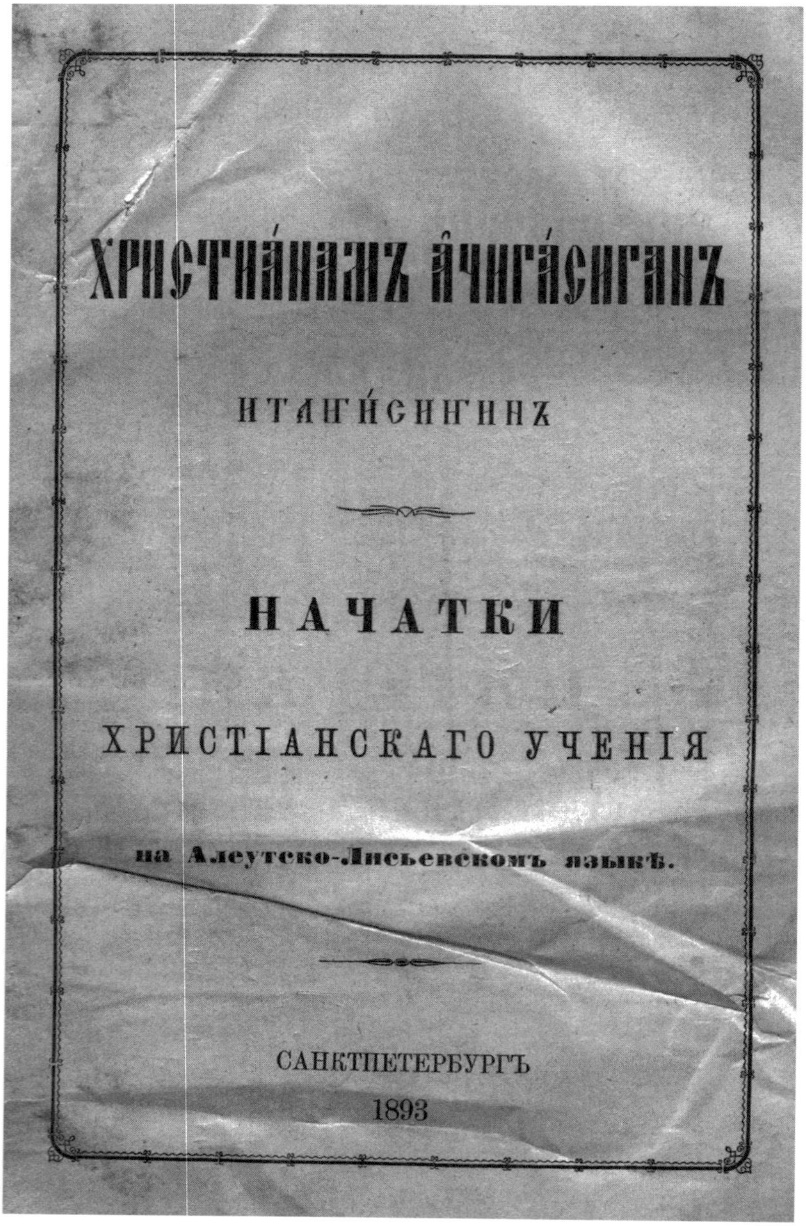

ХРИСТИА́НАМЪ А̂ЧИГА́СИГАНЪ

ИТАНГИ́СИНГИНЪ

НАЧАТКИ

ХРИСТІАНСКАГО УЧЕНІЯ

на Алеутско-Лисьевскомъ языкѣ.

САНКТПЕТЕРБУРГЪ

1893

Cover of a catechism translated into Aleut by St. Innocent, reprinted for the centennial of the establishment of the Orthodox Church in Alaska.

:VIII: Linguist

The Work of St. Innocent for the Native Languages of Alaska and Eastern Siberia[1]

St. Innocent is most often remembered as the pioneer student of, and creator of literacy in, several Alaska Native languages. He was the first to attempt and publish descriptive grammars of the Aleut, Alutiiq, and Tlingit languages. Not too long ago, a scholar dedicated to the preservation and revitalization of Native languages of Alaska wrote:

> During the 120-odd years that the Russians dominated Alaska, the position of Alaska Native languages was not at all weakened, and in several cases considerably strengthened... Those of us who work for the preservation and promotion of this rich, unique Alaskan heritage of Native languages, academically, at the university, educationally in the bilingual programs at the schools, and to some extent also in the churches, are very thankful for the Russian period: for the documentary work done by many Russians, but even more for the precedent they set in their use and cultivation of Alaska Native languages in their churches and schools... This last forty years of Russian America, after the arrival of Veniaminov, I have called a "Golden Age" for Alaskan languages, at least in comparison to what preceded, and especially in comparison to what followed.[2]

Much less known is St. Innocent's work with the Native languages of eastern Siberia and the Russian Far East and his role in developing literacy and literature among the peoples of Yakutia. Suppressed over a period of 75 years, during Communist party rule in Russia, the information is only now being brought out by Yakut scholars.[3]

We must put St. Innocent's work on the languages of the indigenous peoples in the context of his time and his own personal history. As mentioned elsewhere,[4] young Ioann Popov (Veniaminov) grew up in Anga and Irkutsk, in the heart of Mongolian-speaking Buriatia. Moreover, the Irkutsk Seminary, where he studied, had its beginnings as the Mongolian School. Later, when this school became first the Spiritual School (1728) and then the seminary, Mongolian language was taught along with Latin, Greek, Russian and a number of modern European languages. Most important was the fact that the Orthodox Church had a long-standing tradition, stemming from patristic teachings,[5] of instructing peoples in their own languages. When Russians settled in eastern Siberia, the majority of the population became bilingual, and even multilingual, in short order: not only were there persons indigenous to the area who spoke Russian in addition to their own (and often their neighbors') languages, but Russians also communicated in the languages of the regions where they settled.

Thus, from the very beginning of his ministry in Alaska, St. Innocent set himself the task of learning the languages of the people whom he served, creating writing systems and establishing written (and printed) educational and Church literature. He also undertook to provide the scholarly world with information on such languages. His scholarly works, published by the Imperial Academy of Sciences of Russia, and deemed worthy of recognition by special awards, are *Essay on the Grammar of the Eastern Aleut Language* and *Remarks on the Tlingit and Kad'iak languages and also on other languages of Russian America . . .*,[6] both published in 1846. Both works contain vocabularies. The last-mentioned work offers some remarks on classification of languages of the peoples of Alaska and contains the very first attempt in the literature to distinguish the Haida language spoken in the Queen Charlotte Archipelago. Veniaminov, quite correctly, noted that in spite of differences in vocabulary, the structure of the Aleut language was close to that of the language of the Kodiak Archipelago and ". . . if it is correct that the language of Kodiak is a Greenlandic one, then so is the Aleut language."

It is true that modern linguists consider St. Innocent's grammar to have shortcomings in analysis, suffering from the common failing of descriptive linguistics of his time: the application of Indo-European grammatical categories to languages of totally different structures. He was neither a trained philologist nor a trained linguist. Moreover, St. Innocent was a sincerely modest man, and, recognizing the insufficiency of these categories in analyzing the Aleut language, he expressed some doubts and dissatisfaction in this matter only in letters to scholarly friends. On the other hand, his method of eliciting linguistic information cannot be faulted. He always worked with native speakers, preferably those who were bilingual in their own language and Russian, and then checked the information (and his analysis) with other bilinguals. His careful attitude toward linguistic studies is attested in a letter to Admiral F.P. Litke, dated 21 November 1835, Sitka:

> You expect my Tlingit researches. I am ashamed to admit that so far I have undertaken hardly anything; the truth is that I shall be unable to do much which would be *correct*, because I cannot, even if I wish to do so, become as closely acquainted with them as I was with the Fox Islanders. *I lived* with the latter and they opened their soul to me; the Tlingit I can only observe. Therefore, any observations I report would be superficial . . . .[7]

Beginning in 1826, St. Innocent, in cooperation with Aleut friends, notably Ivan Pan'kov, chief of the Krenitzin Islands (Tigalda and Akun), began to produce translations in Aleut. He worked closely with Fr. Iakov Netsvetov, priest of the Atka district of the Russian-American Company, whose native language was Aleut, and for whom Russian was a second language: in the seminary in Irkutsk he had to take special instruction in order to perfect his Russian. Fr. Iakov (now St. Iakov, Enlightener of Alaska Native Peoples) advised St. Innocent on the best use of some of the written symbols derived from the Slavonic and Greek to represent the sounds of the Aleut language. He also checked St. Innocent's translations for accuracy and comprehension. These works include the catechism, the *Gospel of St. Matthew,* to which he added footnotes for Atkans, two sermons never published, and the theological work, *Indication of the Way to the Kingdom of Heaven,* written by St. Innocent originally in Aleut.

A child of his times, St. Innocent was acquainted with the then prevailing philosophy of language: the language of the people represents the essence of their culture, their soul and spirit. Together with Fr. Iakov, he considered whether they should work toward the reduction of dialectal differences between Aleut spoken in different parts of the island chain, so that, through a common language, tribal distinctions would be diminished and subordinated to the Aleuts' need to become one people.

St. Innocent as bishop fostered many individuals who followed in his footsteps: Lavrentii Salamatov, who succeeded Fr. Iakov in the Atka district, wrote an Atkan primer and translated three Gospels into the Atkan dialect of Aleut. Fr. Innokentii Shaiashnikov, who became priest of the Unalaska district in

Father Innokentii Shaiashnikov (1824-1883), priest of Unalaska from 1848 to 1883, one of those who followed St. Innocent in translating biblical works into Alaska Native languages.

Copy of an original photograph, late 1870s, in the possession of Fr. Shaiashnikov's granddaughter, Mrs. Angie Luckhurst of Dillingham, Alaska.

1848, translated into Eastern Aleut all four Gospels (Matthew, Mark, Luke and John), the Acts of the Apostles, a new book of prayers, and several sermons, of which one, against alcoholism, remains very important.

Among the Yup'ik, Fr. Iakov and his students and followers, notably Zakharii Bel'kov and Ioann Orlov, and their successors, continued similar work, while St. Innocent delegated the task of compiling additional material on the Alutiiq and Tlingit languages, and the task of translation into those languages, to seminary students Il'ia Tyzhnov and Ivan Nadezhdin, respectively.

In Yakutia, the translation of religious materials into languages of eastern Siberia began under Veniamin, Bishop of Irkutsk and Nerchinsk, from whose name St. Innocent's surname is derived, and continued under Archbishop Mikhail (Burdukov), St. Innocent's ecclesiastical superior in his early career. The first printed works were prayers in the Yakut and Chukchi languages (1812) and the abridged catechism in Yakut in 1819 (printed in Irkutsk). The translator of the catechism was the priest of the Savior Church in Olekma, Georgii Popov. A new translation of the catechism was done in 1843 by the priest of the St. Nicholas Church in the City of Yakutsk, Mikhail Oshchepkov. This was printed in 1844 in St. Petersburg (Synod Press). However, the flowering of Yakut Church literature is due to the activity of St. Innocent as archbishop, when Yakutia was added to his diocese. He arrived in Yakutsk for the first time in his official capacity in 1852 and almost immediately, by 1853, organized a Translation Committee. The committee was headed by St. Innocent's close friend and coworker, then Archpriest Dimitrii Khitrov (sometimes *Khitrovo*, later the first bishop of the independent Yakutia Diocese, under the monastic name Dionisii). Others were Evsevii Protopopov, Mikhail Oshchepkov, mentioned above, Petr Popov and Dimitrian Popov. By 1854, the committee was supervising translations into the Tungus language, and the compilation of a Tungus-Russian vocabulary and a Tungus grammar.

More than thirty bilingual clergy were involved in this work by the committee. St. Innocent insisted that translations into indigenous languages were needed not so much to teach Christian doctrine, but as a tool to introduce literacy and writing in Native languages.

By 1855, St. Innocent secured permission to print literature in the Yakut language. Father Khitrov was dispatched to St. Petersburg to supervise the printing by the Synod Press in Moscow in 1858: the Gospels, the Acts of the Apostles, and the Old Testament, the Divine Liturgy of John Chrysostom and other church service books (Canons, Book of Hours), St. Innocent's *Indication of the Way to the Kingdom of Heaven*, and a primer and Yakut grammar compiled by Fr. Khitrov. The Yakut primer had a large distribution: 3000 copies were printed, a very large run for the time. Stefan Popov's Tungus primer and a "Short Dictionary" were printed at the same time. By 1869, translations into the Yukagir language were under way. The Lord's prayer was translated anew into the Chukchi language, and also into the Koriak language.

In 1861, under the leadership of St. Innocent, the first printing house in Yakutsk was organized. In 1867, a Yakut-Russian bilingual edition of *Abridged Sacred History* was brought out here, translated by Petr Popov, and the Paschal Divine Service appeared in Yakut. Other works followed soon thereafter. In the same period, St. Innocent initiated work in the languages of Southern Tungus speaking peoples. His daughter-in-law, Ekaterina Veniaminov, learned the Negidal and Nanai languages so that she could work with the women. Unfortunately, no information has come to light so far on the results of his efforts in respect to those Native languages of the Amur region.

The work of translation, and publication, in indigenous languages of eastern Siberia and Alaska was continued after the death of St. Innocent by the Orthodox Missionary Society he founded and by the Kazan' Pedagogical Seminary where a Translation Commission was established in accordance with the urging of St. Innocent expressed as Metropolitan of Moscow. In 1899, a new and expanded Yakut Translation Commission was formed under the auspices of the Missionary Society. More than 60 works were published in the Yakut language alone before 1916. St. Innocent's contribution is characterized by modern Yakut scholars as being "beyond price." Yakut spiritual literature, published in the nineteenth century, is considered "...the first experience in national book publishing and forms one of the most important stages in the history and culture of the people of Yakutia."

This year, Yakutia has joined Alaska in celebrating the legacy of a remarkable man, scholar, and linguist.

Order of St. Anna, received by St. Innocent in 1840.

Order of St. Alexander Nevskii sash, badge, and star, awarded to St. Innocent in 1862.

Notes

1 In this account we rely most heavily, for the languages of Alaska, on the work of Michael E. Krauss, Director, Alaska Native Language Center, University of Alaska Fairbanks, specifically, *Alaska Native Languages: Past, Present and Future*, Research Paper no. 4 (Fairbanks: Alaska Native Language Center, 1980) and "Alaska Native Languages in Russian America" in *Russian America: The Forgotten Frontier*, edited by Barbara Sweetland Smith and Redmond J. Barnett (Tacoma, Washington: Washington State Historical Society, 1990), 205-213. For information on St. Innocent's work in the languages of eastern Siberia, we are indebted to Evdokiia Pavlovna Guliaieva, Curator of Rare Books, National Library of the Republic of Sakha (Yakutia), especially her paper "Knigoizdatel'skaia deiatel'nost' russkoi pravoslavnoi missii v Yakutii (1812-1916 gg.)" [Book publication activities of the Russian Orthodox mission in Yakutia, 1816-1916], presented at Edinburgh, 19 April 1997, and "Church Translations into Native Languages of Yakutia," presented 15 April 1997 at the International Symposium to Commemorate the Bicentennial of the Birth of Innokentii Veniaminov, Pembroke College, Oxford University, England, 14–15 April 1997.

Order of St. Vladimir, awarded to St. Innocent in 1867.

Order of St. Andrew, received by St. Innocent in 1872.

---

2 Krauss 1990:205, 211.

3 Foremost among them, E.P. Guliaieva and Egor Spiridonovich Shishigin.

4 See the essay "A Very Human Story," this volume.

5 Patristic teachings are the teachings of the writers of the early Church, that is, the Church of the first four centuries A.D., from Justin to Cyril of Alexandria. These writers laid the foundation for the developing Christian, especially Orthodox, theology. Of great importance is the teaching that Divine revelation is, in essence, open to all peoples, Christian and non-Christian alike. It is no accident that the International Symposium to Commemorate the Birth of Innokentii Veniaminov, held at Pembroke College, Oxford University, 14–15 April 1997, was entitled "Bishop Innokentii and the Greek Patristic Background."

6 *Opyt grammatiki aleutsko-lis'evskago iazyka* and *Zamechaniia o koloshenskom i kad'iakskom iazykakh i otchasti o prochikh rossiisko-amerikanskikh, s prisovokupleniem rossiisko-koloshenskago slovaria, soderzhashchee bolee 1000 slov, iz koikh na nekotorye sdelany poiasneniia.*

7 Emphasis in original.

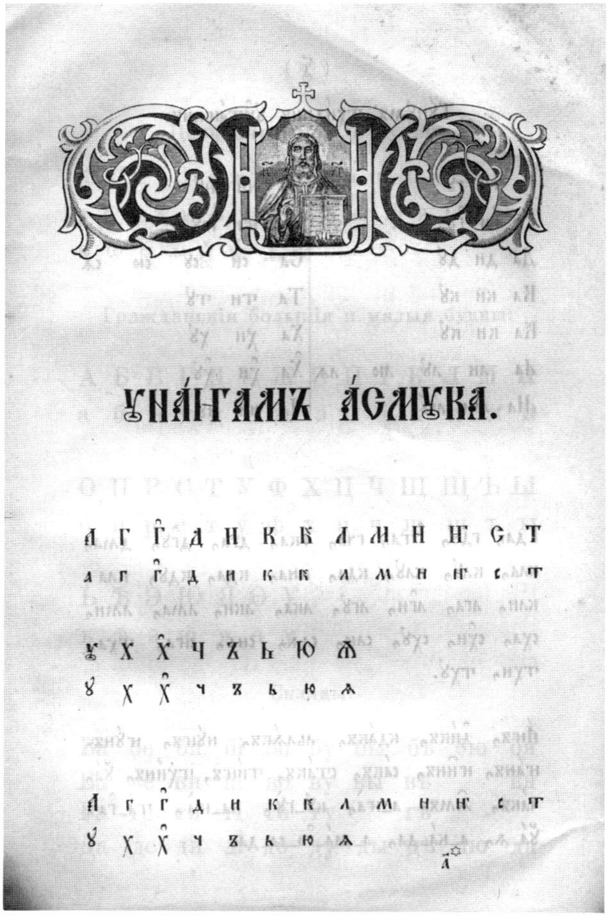

Aleut primer.

:IX: Educator[1]

Education was St. Innocent's lifelong passion. A brilliant student, he read voraciously, in many fields, from natural science to theology and philosophy, constantly borrowing books from the Russian-American Company's library in Sitka and from friends. Nothing gave him more pleasure than the arrival of new publications from Russia.

His devotion to and respect for learning, and early recognition of the value of education, soon resulted in advocacy of educational opportunities for all and development of a then innovative philosophy of education that today appears fully modern. Teaching became another passion, second only to his appreciation of learning.

In his view, education had to combine pursuit of knowledge with ethics and morality. "Among the people, literacy without ethics may be likened to a knife in the hands of a willful child," he wrote. Educated strata, devoid of morals and ethics, are dangerous and destructive, he continued. He believed that the best educators were parents. Therefore, the first task was to ensure that all parents were educated in the true sense of the word, as he understood it.

How to achieve this ideal of universal education when, in his time, schools were few and many people lacked educational opportunities? Teach, teach from the very beginning, teach children from the earliest age, as young as two years old (today we would say he advocated Headstart). Teach everyone, especially children of the ordinary folk. Pastors of the church flock should fill the void. St. Innocent burned with the wish to implement his ideas. He wrote:

> To teach! A beautiful and widespread idea; but is it possible to implement it universally?
>
> Such thoughts I conceived while still in Irkutsk and I presented my ideas to the then archpastor Michael, as a proposal. He liked it and instructed all city clergy to follow the proposal as I outlined.

> But none of my brethren did so, I failed to find among my fellows, with the exception of one deacon, those who thought in the same way, who would have supported me and aided me . . . . [T]he Lord rewarded me, though: I began to wish to go to America. One of my first thoughts was that I shall be able to act there on my own and teach in the way I wish! I thank God that during my entire stay in America I acted upon this to the utmost of my ability.

St. Innocent expressed his thoughts by the following categories, which we summarize here. Who is to be taught? All. What is to be taught? Piety. How to teach? The best method is a simple conversation or story telling. Where to teach? Anywhere, no special structure is necessary, the church can serve. Who is to teach? Clergy, celebrants and servitors both. When to teach? In the beginning, on feast days and holidays, at least fifty times per year. By what (financial) means? Almost none, most needed are rewards for learning. How to motivate clergy to teach? Make it their duty, and ensure that they carry it out through supervision by deans of clergy. How to motivate children to learn? Not through compulsion at all, but by explaining to parents the aims and importance of such education. What obstacles may one encounter? If one approaches the problem as a matter of state aimed at salvation of souls and enlightenment of the population, which lead to great benefit for the homeland, no obstacle will be insurmountable. Will such a program bring any benefits? Yes, not right away, but, he wrote, "surely within 15 years, and in 20 Russia would be transformed! A new educated generation will have been created. And seeing the fruits of their labors, the teachers-clergy will themselves be uplifted. I know this from experience. I knew, before I started teaching, that faith brings spiritual solace, but I knew that theoretically only. But the Lord blessed me and permitted me to partake of such solace when I began teaching. Truly, the saying is right: as you teach, you learn!"

St. Innocent firmly believed that the first teachers of a child are the parents. Hence, the education of adults should never be neglected. Especially important in the child's life is a good mother. Therefore, women should be educated as well as men.

In Alaska, and later in eastern Asiatic Russia, St. Innocent saw to it that a school was organized wherever a church or chapel was established. In Alaska, we know several outstanding teachers who followed St. Innocent's precepts and passed the same to the next generation of St. Innocent's fosterlings: Fr. Iakov

Netsvetov, Deacon Vasilii Shishkin, Fr. Innokentii Shaiashnikov and his wife, Maria, Fr. Pavel Shaiashnikov, Fr. Lavrentii Salamatov, Fr. Moses Salamatov and his daughter Matrena Salamatov, Fr. Innokentii Lestenkov, Frs. Peter F. and Peter P. Kashevarov, Fr. Vasilii Kashevarov, and Fr. Nikolai Kashevarov. These and many others, some remembered, some forgotten, carried on the educational work started by St. Innocent as a young priest at Unalaska, even into the twentieth century.

The best known formal schools that St. Innocent established in Alaska, Yakutia, and the Russian Far East, are spiritual schools and seminaries. The seminary established at Novoarkhangel'sk became a renowned institution where Native languages were taught; where instruction was always bilingual, and after 1867 trilingual (English was incorporated into the curriculum); and the future clergy were trained in making a living from the land, in navigation and the handling of small water craft, and in the basics of medicine and public health practices. Clergy became responsible for vaccination against smallpox and often were instrumental in establishing and maintaining medical aid stations. In 1879, Fr. Innokentii Shaiashnikov was instrumental in organizing a new hospital at Unalaska. He also started publishing a paper, which eventually printed news and opinion in three languages: Aleut, Russian, and English. In the village "schools" – often held in the clerics' homes– these devoted men and women strove to maintain and preserve their Native language literacy, a literacy created initially by St. Innocent for Aleut, Alutiiq and Tlingit and carried by his fosterlings to Yup'ik and Athabaskan peoples of Alaska.

As archbishop and metropolitan, St. Innocent fostered establishment of spiritual schools and academies for women. He also established, and encouraged others to establish, scholarships for children of clergy, peasants, and other poor strata of Russian society, not only to the spiritual schools but also to universities. As Metropolitan of Moscow and Kolomna, he established a school of iconography, as well as a museum of Orthodox iconography, in Moscow. At least ten scholarships to this school were created.

St. Innocent also supported establishment of vocational educational institutions in which crafts were taught.

His vision of the goals of universal education was far ahead of his times. Perhaps he could not shape the Russian educational system in accordance with his ideals, but these ideals have not lost their relevance and should be studied and appreciated today.

Notes

[1] Based on a letter to Count Protasov, Holy Ruling Synod, dated 2 July 1845 at Petropavlovsk (Letters of Metropolitan Innocent, *Pis'ma Innokentiia Mitropolita Moskovskago i Kolomenskago*, vol. 1 [St. Petersburg: Synod Press, 1897], pp. 138-152, letter No. 56) and additional references in letters to friends and in St. Innocent's papers.

:X: Craftsman and Inventor

St. Innocent was skilled in several crafts and in some achieved mastery.

His first teacher was his uncle Dimitrii (later Hieromonk David), who excelled in woodworking, metal work, and clock making. In later life, when St. Innocent was responsible for a huge diocese, crafts provided him much-needed enjoyment, relaxation, and relief from stress.

Cartographer and draftsman. St. Innocent was an excellent draftsman and cartographer. He studied draftsmanship in the seminary. In 1828, he made a hand-sketched chart of the Eastern Aleutians which was used by F.P. Litke in compiling his atlas and is featured in the exhibit.[1] In 1831, he sent Kiril Khlebnikov a map, or rather chart, of the Unalaska district, indicating all settlements. St. Innocent felt, however, that this hand-drawn map was not sufficiently precise and should serve only as a souvenir.

Architect and builder. In 1824, St. Innocent designed the Church of the Holy Ascension of Christ in Unalaska, which replaced the small octagonal chapel built in 1807. He personally supervised the construction of this church. He actively participated in design and construction of the St. Michael Cathedral in Sitka and of the Church of the Holy Resurrection[2] in Sitka that he had built for the Tlingit Christian community. It is believed that he also took part in designing the Bishop's House in Sitka, now a museum under the auspices of the U. S. National Park Service. He always reviewed plans for new churches built in his diocese, inspecting the proposals with a critical and educated eye. As Metropolitan of Moscow, he took active part in the architectural development of his summer residence in Moscow, Cherkizovo.

Carpenter and joiner. St. Innocent was an able carpenter and joiner. For example, soon after his arrival in Unalaska in 1824, he built, with the help of his brother Stephan, a house for his family. He particularly enjoyed woodworking. As a young deacon, St. Innocent made various items for the Church of the Annunciation in Irkutsk (for example, a skillfully made storage case for the candelabra used in the Easter services) and it is said that he also made with his own hands the altar tables and tables of oblation for almost all the churches built and consecrated in his diocese.[3] One example of his woodworking is believed to be a small and highly functional lap desk, which could efficiently be used for writing when traveling.[4]

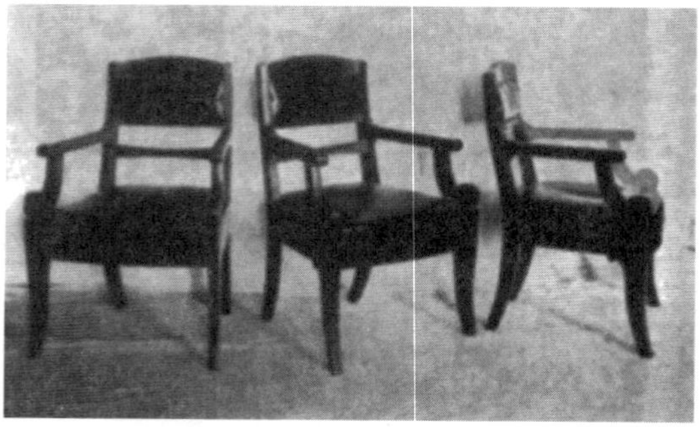

Chairs (above) and a clock (below) made by St. Innocent.

Furniture maker. St. Innocent is best known for furniture making, as many examples survive, especially in Alaska. It is said that while at Unalaska he made all the furniture and interior features in the house he built for his family.[5] At least one example of furniture made by St. Innocent, an easy chair of ash, with springs, upholstered in dark velvet, with ladder back of baleen, found its way into the Church Archaeological Museum at the Spiritual Academy of Kiev. It was at one time owned by St. Innocent's friend, A.N. Murav'iev, who stated that this chair was made by St. Innocent in 1830, that is, while he still was living at Unalaska.

Maker of clocks and precision instruments. Clock- and precision instrument making always fascinated St. Innocent. While still a seminarian, he assisted a master clock maker in building the bell tower clock at the cathedral in Irkutsk. In Alaska, he designed and built the bell tower clock for the St. Michael Cathedral in Sitka. He is known to have made several grandfather clocks and desk clocks, one of which survived until recently in Sitka. He loved watches, and often repaired these for friends. Captain Edward Belcher, commanding H.M.S. *Sulphur*, visited St. Innocent's workshop when in Sitka in 1837. There Belcher noted ". . . a good barrel organ, a barometer, and several other articles of his own manufacture. He was kind enough to volunteer his services on one or two of our sick barometers, and succeeded effectually." Midshipman Simpkinson, also of the *Sulphur*, wrote in his journal: "He understands regarding mathematical instruments, sextants &c. and as a proof of this we sent him several of our barometers (which had been broken) to repair. He also made the only musical instrument which [we] had to dance to, a small hand organ. . . ."[6] In 1864, as archbishop,

St. Innocent ordered from Moscow binoculars, barometers, and thermometers he needed for weather observation. Noting that he himself used to make thermometers, he found those delivered to him wanting: placed next to each other, the instruments showed marked divergences in recorded temperature. He noted that one of those thermometers did not function at temperatures below zero and that the scale was not the standard Reaumur one. He demanded to know if this was an innovation based on a new theory and if such had been accepted by the Academy of Sciences.[7]

Organ builder. St. Innocent loved music, and constructing musical instruments. In this avocation he is best known for the hand organs he began building while still in Irkutsk. While at Unalaska, he built organs for sale in the California missions. From his letters to Kiril Khlebnikov, who sold the organs for him, it is evident that he built these on order:

> . . . if the padres desire to have another organ, with their own music, tell them it will be ready in a year; it will be of the same size and with two rollers. In such a case, please be good enough to bring from them music in the same notation as the music I am sending with this organ; also please send to me some mahogany for veneer or a box, securely constructed and veneered. And dry aromatic wood for the channel. If possible, have cast for me an organ key with all the appurtenances, even if it were not turned and lacking screws. My organ is on its way to you and I have supplied Grigorii Klimovich [Terent'iev] with full written instructions on how the organ should be handled.

The organs were priced at 500 "piasters or marks" or up to 40 pud (ca. 1,440 lbs) of grain for bread.[8]

When working as a "mechanic," St. Innocent often found that needed materials were lacking. In such situations, he used whatever was handy. It is said that he used the blade of a knife to fashion a part for the bell tower clock of the Sitka cathedral. A good craftsman himself, he always respected manual work and the craftsmanship of others.

Notes

1 A copy of this chart was provided by the Navy Archive of Russia, St. Petersburg.

2 This church in later literature began to be referred to as the Church of the Holy Trinity.

[3] Testimony of Fr. Strukov, pastor of the Church of the Annunciation in Irkutsk in the 1870s, in Barsukov's biography of St. Innocent (1883), p. 734.

[4] This desk is on loan to the national park in Sitka courtesy of the Sheldon Jackson Museum, one of the two Alaska State Museums.

[5] One item is in the Baranoff Museum in Kodiak, and several items are in Sitka (U.S. National Park Service).

[6] R.A. Pierce and J. H. Winslow, editors, *H.M.S. Sulphur on the Northwest and California Coasts, 1837 and 1839* (Kingston, Ontario: The Limestone Press, 1979), 23, 103.

[7] For St. Innocent's theoretical discussion of the deficiencies he saw in the thermometers, and the defects in the barometer which he ascribed to incorrect packaging, see Barsukov's biography, *Innokentii, Mitropolit Moskovskii i Kolomenskii . . .* (1883), pp. 531-533.

[8] A.D. Drizdo and R. V. Kinzhalov, compilers and editors, *Russkaia Amerika . . .*, (Moscow: Mysl', 1994), 166, 167.

:XI: Scholar

St. Innocent's scholarly reputation today rests largely on his ethnographic work in Alaska.[1] Foremost is his famous book, *Notes on the Islands of the Unalashka District*,[2] which contains his own observations on Eastern Aleut culture and Fr. Iakov Netsvetov's notes on the culture of the Atka (Central) Aleuts. A brief outline of the Tlingit culture and beliefs, based on St. Innocent's observations, is also presented. However, this book is much more than an ethnography. Part one is devoted entirely to what today we would consider an ecological description of the Eastern Aleutian area of settlement from the Alaska Peninsula to the Islands of Four Mountains and of the Pribilof Islands. It

Chart of the eastern Aleutian Islands by St. Innocent (1828).

Reproduction courtesy of the State Navy Archive of Russia (GAVMF), Catalog No. 1894.

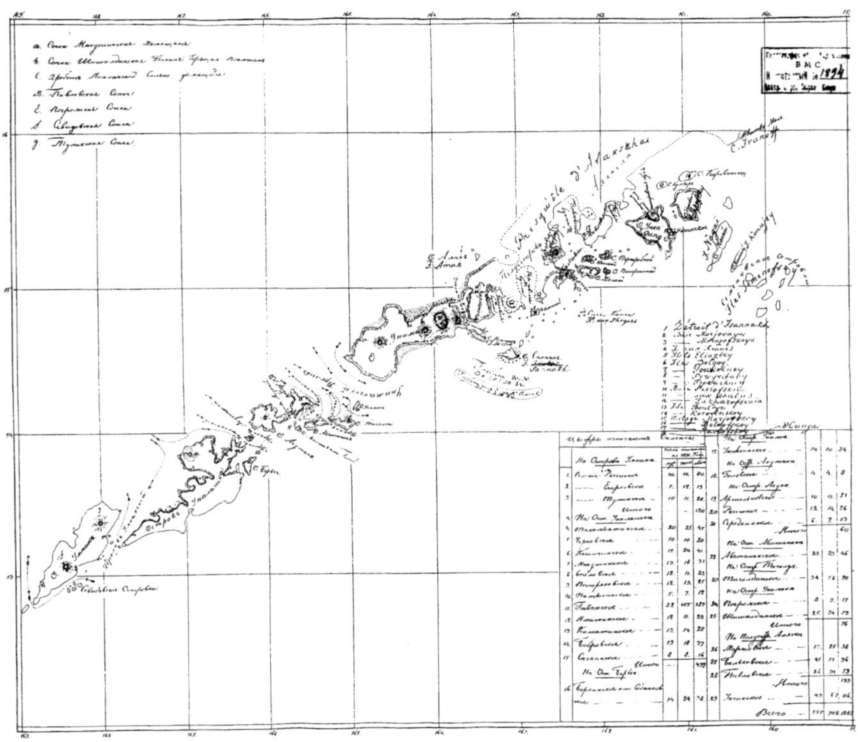

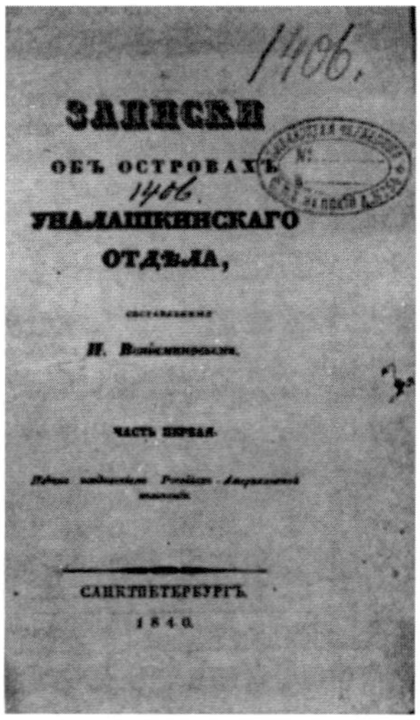

Title page of the original 1840 edition of St. Innocent's Notes on the Islands of the Unalashka District.

should be noted that, in his scholarly work, St. Innocent always preferred to write about matters he knew first hand. Moreover, two special sections in the book are devoted to the description of land and marine fauna (including fish), their distribution, a pioneering essay on whales, and the ways in which they were utilized by the Aleuts as well as the Russians. St. Innocent includes statistics on the fur seal take from 1817 through 1837 in the Pribilof Islands. The work also advocates the necessity of conservation practices. These sections of the book reflect his interests in environmental studies, to which we shall return below. Here, we draw the reader's attention to the fact that St. Innocent was the first to collect Aleut and Tlingit folklore, analyze the marriage rules affecting certain categories of kin among the Aleuts,[3] and publish a number of ethnographic articles in a variety of Russian journals. Among the latter is an almost unknown article on the role of Tlingit women. Unfortunately, this material has never been translated into English.

St. Innocent had a lifelong interest in natural sciences. He studied the environment as a whole and was extremely sensitive to the importance of micro-environmental variation for human survival. However, he was also able to focus on specifics: geology, meteorology, ocean studies, and so on. An acute observer, he noted extraordinary occurrences and, when possible, collected specimens to substantiate his observations. While at Unalaska, he collected geological specimens (rocks and minerals) which he sent to Kiril Khlebnikov in Sitka. He noted the existence of beach ridges, today used as geological time markers to date coastal archaeological sites, and postulated certain changes in sea level over time. In this, St. Innocent based his reasoning on observation of fossilized shells high above current sea level on both the Pacific and Bering Sea shores of the Alaska Peninsula, and of newly formed lowlands covered with vegetation. He made similar observations in the Shumagin Islands. He noted finds of mammoth tusks and bones and the soil conditions where such finds occur. He subscribed to the hypothesis that at one time the Asian and American continents were joined, a hypothesis today accepted as fact: the Bering Land Bridge.

St. Innocent studied the occurrence and condition of sea ice, both shore and floating, noting the fluctuations. He kept records of winds, tides, currents and their changes, barometric pressure, precipitation, etc. In short, he acted as meteorological observer. He provides us with the earliest systematic record of volcanic and seismic activity in southwestern Alaska. He was the first to describe the petrified forest on Unga Island and, as far as we know, the first to record coal deposits on that island.

St. Innocent engaged in such activities during his travels as well as in regions where he resided later. Unfortunately, we have no record of his ecological observations on Kamchatka,[4] but his extensive position paper on the Amur region[5] survives and testifies that even at an advanced age he remained the same enthusiastic scholar of natural sciences as he was in his youth in Alaska.

Notes

1 For his contribution to the study of Alaska Native languages, see the special essay on that topic, this volume.

2 First published in Russian in 1840, it appeared in English only in 1984, translated by Lydia T. Black and R.H. Geoghegan, edited and with an introduction by Richard A. Pierce (Kingston, Ontario: The Limestone Press).

3 This information is contained in a report to Archbishop Michael of Irkutsk and Nerchinsk. On this subject see Patricia A. Petrivelli, "Aleut Kinship System," work in progress.

4 The bulk of his notes perished in the 1850s in the fire at the Savior Monastery in Yakutsk.

5 *Nechto ob Amure*, published by Barsukov after St. Innocent's death.

St. Innocent, shortly before his death.

Courtesy of the State Museum of Yakutsk.

:XII: Through Others' Eyes

Today, when thousands of people around the world venerate St. Innocent and pray for his intercession before the Almighty God, it is seldom remembered what kind of a man he was. We forget that he laughed and cried, occasionally lost his temper, loved, had close friends with whom he shared his joys and sorrows, suffered and endured.

St. Innocent was a man of imposing physique and striking appearance. Foreigners who visited Sitka invariably were impressed by his stature, for he was well over six feet tall. "A very powerful athletic man," wrote Captain Edward Belcher, who met St. Innocent in 1837 and was very much taken with him. Sir George Simpson, of the Hudson's Bay Company, encountered St. Innocent in 1841 and 1842 when the latter resided at Novoarkhangel'sk as bishop.[2] The worldly, sophisticated, and widely traveled Simpson had this to say about him:

> This prelate's diocese is perhaps the most extensive in existence, comprising, as it does, not only the whole of Russian America, but also the Sea of Ochotsk [*sic*], Kamschatka [*sic*] and the Aleutian archipelagos. He looks as if intended by Nature for the bishopric of two worlds, being a man of Herculean frame; and the specimen of his travels, which I have just mentioned, shows that he is likely to need all his constitution for an episcopal visitation.[3]

In his travels, St. Innocent did not expect conveniences. Prone to sea sickness, he nevertheless traveled by kayak, boat, or ship whenever duty called. He ate what was on hand and took minimum supplies and provisions.

St. Innocent had been accustomed to endure since childhood. Though his early years were spent with his loving family, material conditions were poor, to say the least. When he entered the seminary, the regime there was spartan. Food was of the simplest, and poor in quality. St. Innocent once remarked that he did not taste rye bread without chaff until he left the seminary. Discipline was severe. St. Innocent early learned self control.

Much later, one of the clergymen on the Amur remarked that St. Innocent "did not jump for joy, and saw misfortunes as the inevitable lot of humanity."

But, St. Innocent also learned compassion and tolerance for human failings. He seldom, if ever, raised his voice when dealing with recalcitrant subordinates. He was tolerant even of those who themselves were intolerant by nature. Years later, writing to a friend about his former Bishop Vicar Petr, who was on his way to a remote monastery by order of ecclesiastical superiors, St. Innocent commented: "this will be good for him; perhaps there he will finally learn that angels are not to be found among human beings." Incidentally, this was his only overt criticism of this rather unsatisfactory subordinate. Sir George Simpson's remarks are apropos here:

> On taking leave of this worthy prelate I cannot refrain from rendering a small tribute of praise to his character and qualifications; and as he is still in the prime of life, I trust that his widely scattered flock may long enjoy the benefit of those powers of mind and body which combine to fit him for his important and arduous charge. His appearance, to which I already alluded, impresses a stranger with something of awe, while on further intercourse the gentleness which characterizes his every word and deed insensibly molds reverence into love, and at the same time his talents and attainments are such as to be well worthy of his exalted station. With all this, the bishop is sufficiently a man of the world to disdain anything like cant. His conversation, on the contrary, teems with amusement and instruction, and his company is much prized by all who have the honor of his acquaintance.

St. Innocent, indeed, could speak well (even Simpson remarked on the attention with which his flock listened to his sermons). His command of language was excellent and he frequently used Russian folk proverbs. Once, he characterized a fellow bishop as a fine pastor except when he went after a fly with an axe. His sense of humor was wicked, the jokes delivered deadpan. Even in his old age, as metropolitan, he enjoyed a joke. Russians have a saying, when referring to someone who talks about a subject in ignorance, that this person's understanding is like that of pigs when confronted with oranges. St. Innocent rose to the defense of pigs. Well, he said, when I was traveling around the world I had occasion to observe pigs, especially in Tahiti where they are many. The pigs there do not lack any fruit–but I noted that they invariably went for the oranges. Hence, pigs are discerning creatures.[4] St. Innocent, apparently, did not like bathos. In one instance, discussing a very tragic case which bothered him greatly, he phrased the news as news of earthquakes: the first, a real one, he reports, happened on 18 March (1848), the second was "the quake that shook the house of the Kashevarovs."[5] In a lighter vein, when traveling to Aian, occupied by the English during the Crimean War, he responded to his daughter's caution: "They do not need me. If they take me, they will have to feed me," implying that feeding his great frame would be very expensive. St. Innocent was fond of using nicknames. In letters to friends he often refers to mutual acquaintances by such. For example, his favorite Bishop Vicar of Yakutsk (later of Alaska), Pavel (Paul Popov), is referred to as "He of Many Words."[6]

St. Innocent was a fervent believer in the significance of dreams. He believed that dreams often foretold the future and made the hidden known. In many letters he recounts his or others' dreams and wonders how to interpret such dreams correctly.

St. Innocent was never greedy. While in Alaska, he never accepted recompense for priestly services, such as baptisms or funerals, from his parishioners. As bishop, and archbishop, he discouraged subordinate clergy from following this age-old practice, preferring instead to assign them substantially higher salaries. When, as a prelate, his income was substantial, he freely gave to the churches and to organizations that supported the poor, and gave scholarships. He did not seek riches and did not expect his children to strive for material advancement. He once wrote to his youngest daughter, Fekla, not to be arrogant, as she would never be a countess nor would she ever be rich, as he was not able to provide a dowry. He urged his daughter Paraskeva, who had taken the monastic veil, to share her inheritance with her much poorer sister Catherine and destitute brother Innokentii. The inheritance willed to him by his daughter Olga he gave away, to his children, to the poor, and to the Greek churches. On the other hand, he did not consider poverty a virtue. When as a young man he saved some capital by selling products of his craftsmanship, he invested it in a gold mining enterprise and was very pleased when this investment bore fruit. The proceeds he divided between donations to the Church, mostly in his native Anga, and support for the families of his sisters and of his mother's relatives. He understood the realities of life. He was an effective fund raiser for his diocese, the schools, and charitable causes close to his heart. As a fund raiser, he was not at all bashful.

St. Innocent was a loyal friend and never forgot those who helped him along the way, especially those who were good to him in his youth. When, as bishop, he visited Irkutsk and his former teachers at the seminary, especially the aged dean, bowed to the ground before him, he raised the latter, embraced him, and said: "Not you before me, but I before you must bow; it is because of you that I became what I am."[7] He was no less loyal to his former classmates and to his colleagues who served as priests in Alaska. Occasionally, however, he did voice his disappointments, especially when he felt that the clergy whom he fostered in Alaska were in some ways letting him down. Often, he wrote to the relatives of his subordinates serving in remote places in order to bring them news and reassure them about their loved ones. Opposed to revolutionary movements on principle, he nevertheless consoled relatives of exiled Decembrists. His attitude toward his family we discuss elsewhere in this volume.[8] Here we shall mention only his unwavering moral support for his children, especially evident in letters to his daughter Paraskeva upon her decision to become a nun, and later when she faced difficulties in following the monastic path.

St. Innocent was always modest. When he, already a bishop, was in Petropavlovsk on Kamchatka where an earthquake severely damaged the cathedral, he took part in the repair work and himself, experienced carpenter that he was, fixed the altar table. He entertained simply, without pretense. On one occasion, when his name day (the feast of St. John) was being celebrated in company with two former seminarians, now priests, instead of receiving gifts he gave gifts to his guests: the Gospel of St. Matthew in the Aleut language.

Perhaps this character trait is best expressed in several of his letters to daughter Paraskeva, the nun Mother Poliksenia:

> You ask my advice how to seek salvation. Oh my Pashen'ka! I myself am ready to ask your counsel how I am to seek it. My learning began long ago, but I am still learning the primer; occasionally, it seems, I reach the syllable level, but then I look and find I have forgotten almost all and start again with the primer. To understand the Gospels–God alone knows if I ever shall reach that level.

And a decade later, in 1863, he wrote to Poliksenia: "I am unable to teach you the monastic life, as I never was an ordinary monk. Therefore, I have no experience how to live under the vow of obedience. Such things may be taught only by those who have experienced them."

His old classmate, Archpriest Prokopii Gromov, contrasted the young priest celebrating services in a tent, where the congregation consisted of Native men, women and children, with the services St. Innocent held in the Dormition Cathederal in Moscow, where Russian tsars were crowned. But the character of the man did not change. St. Innocent himself wrote: "Am I good, or am I bad–whatever I am, I have no intention to change or reform myself; who I was before, thus I remain." Indeed, the evidence we have on hand shows that St. Innocent to the end of his days remained true to himself: a kind, considerate human being, grateful for gifts given to him and willing to give to others as long as he had being.

Notes

1 Material in this essay, unless otherwise cited, is based primarily on data in Barsukov's biography of St. Innocent (*Innokentii, Mitropolit Moskovskii i Kolomenskii...*, 1883), and St. Innocent's letters (Barsukov, compiler, 1897-1901, 3 vols.). For biographies of St. Innocent in English, see Charles R. Hale, *Innocent of Moscow, the Apostle of Kamchatka and Alaska* (privately printed, 1877) and a more recent one, written following the glorification of Innokentii (Veniaminov) as a Saint of the Russian Orthodox Church, by Paul D. Garrett, *St. Innocent, Apostle to America* (New York: Athens Printing Company for St. Vladimir Seminary Press, 1979).

2 One of the officers aboard Simpson's vessel *Cowlitz* sketched a portrait of St. Innocent. Later, while in the Amur region, St. Innocent sent this portait or sketch to Nikolai D. Sverbeev. (*Pis'ma . . .* , vol.1, p. 343).

3 This and the following quote are from Sir George Simpson's *Narrative of A Journey Round the World during the Years 1841 and 1842* (London: Henry Colburn Publisher, 1847), 180, 191.

4 Paraphrased after quote in Barsukov's biography (1883), pp. 105-106.

5 This refers to the infanticide of a child born out of wedlock, committed by a female member of the Kashevarov family. The infant's grandmother, of Alutiiq origin and widow of Filip Kashevarov, the family's founder, dismembered the body (in the Alutiiq world view dismemberment of those dead by violence prevented the soul from haunting the living; they were then truly dead). From the clerical point of view, the event was aggravated by the fact that both the mother and grandmother of the murdered infant continued to participate in communion and baked communion bread.

6 *Mnogoglagol'nyi* in Russian. The term is derived from Slavonic.

7 Barsukov, biography (1883), p. 142.

8 See "A Very Human Story," in this volume.

St. Innocent as Metropolitan of Moscow with his son Archpriest Gavriil I. Veniaminov and one of his two grandsons, Evsevii G. Veniaminov.

Reproduced from *Notes on the Unalashka District* (Kingston, Ontario: The Limestone Press, 1984).

:XIII: A Very Human Story

Son, Brother, Husband, Father[1]

St. Innocent, in his correspondence available in print, rarely refers directly to his married life. His affection for his wife can only be inferred from oblique references in a few letters to friends, but especially in letters to his daughters, and from the way in which he observed her memory after her death. It is remarkable how often he refers to the sad situation of married women who bear children year after year, to the grief over children who die in infancy, to being careworn with household duties. He was eloquent on this point when writing to his daughter Paraskeva, who decided to become a nun but then had doubts about her choice. "Look at the others," he wrote. "Not many joys fall to their lot! It seems they are happy until the first child comes; then follow endless cares, worries, sadness and sorrows. . . ." In 1852, he again raised this point:

> I wrote you that your elder sister envies your present state–and this even when she has a husband who is mild, with whom she had no cross word for 13 years, and the children are healthy and intelligent. Yet, she thinks you are happier than she. She has nowadays so many cares, for her husband, children, her home, and about the future as well as about her soul. And in time there will be even more concerns. How many fears she has about the future! You, my little friend, have none of these and will not have such cares in the future. . . . You may have many children–I mean good deeds and prayer–those, thy children, will never trouble you, but will give you solace and joy; they will never be sick and they shall never die, they will not become orphans at your death, they shall follow you to the grave. . . .

Many times he expressed his conviction that educated, morally strong women bring up children well prepared for life. Mothers, wrote St. Innocent, are the best educators, ever.

A good example of his attitude toward women is his appreciation of his daughter-in-law Ekaterina, wife of his son Gavriil. According to St. Innocent, she was rather unprepossessing in appearance (he was disappointed in her looks when he first met her), but had a good sense of family, loved learning, and evidenced strong moral fiber.

Moreover, his care for his mother and, after her death, concern for her relatives, and the care for his married sisters and their children, testify to the respect he had especially for hardworking peasant women. The reasons for his concerns lie in his personal and his family's history.

By 1824, when St. Innocent was preparing to go to Alaska, his wife Ekaterina (Catherine) had borne him four children, of whom only one, the infant son Innokentii (born 1823), survived. At the time of the trip she was again pregnant. One can only imagine how she coped with the months-long travel by horse and river barge, and then by sailing vessel not equipped for carrying passengers needing special care and lacking many conveniences.[2]

Perhaps it was a consolation that her mother-in-law, Fekla, traveled with them and in Alaska often acted as midwife and helped with the care of the children. Ioann's two sisters, whose names we do not know at this point, were by this time married. But Stephan, aged twenty, like his brother schooled in usages of the Church, also accompanied the family and would serve his brother as sub-deacon and the second teacher in the school at Unalaska.

The family set out from Irkutsk in horse-drawn carts, stopping first of all in their native Anga, where Fr. Ioann celebrated a *moleben* (Te Deum) in the Church of St. Elias that his father and uncle had served. From there they traveled on the Lena River to Yakutsk, and from Yakutsk to Okhotsk on horseback. At Okhotsk, they boarded a vessel of the Russian-American Company for Sitka Island. Their first surviving daughter, named for her mother Catherine, was born aboard the vessel.

The family's first winter in Alaska was spent at Novoarkhangel'sk (Sitka), where Fr. Ioann concelebrated with Fr. Aleksei Sokolov, taught school, and began to study the Aleut language. Next navigational season they sailed for their final destination, Unalaska in the Eastern Aleutian Islands. They arrived at Unalaska on 29 July 1824, having spent over twenty-eight days at sea. Nevertheless, the first thing that "our ladies" did, wrote St. Innocent, was berry picking: the day was sunny and mild, a rare occurrence, as they soon learned.

The living conditions at Unalaska were primitive compared to Irkutsk: the family's house was a semisubterranean one with no amenities. The salary the young priest received was insufficient to support his numerous dependents. Soon, to supplement his income, he was building musical instruments for sale. Then, Fr. Ioann, with the help of his brother Stephan, built a Russian-style house for his family and furnished it with furniture he himself made. He even made a wall clock.

His family continued to grow. Two more sons, Gavriil (Gabriel) and Aleksandr (Alexander) were born at Unalaska in 1826 and 1827, followed by three girls, Olga (1829), Paraskeva (1830) and Fekla (1832), the youngest child, whom St. Innocent called by an Aleut nickname "kucha," the little one, which he modified in Russian to "Kusha" and "Kushen'ka." Concerned with the need to educate the children, and about his wife's health, he began to ask to be relieved of his duties by not later than 1831 and for permission to return to Russia.

As he was not permitted to leave before a suitable replacement was found, in 1832 he sent his two older boys, Innokentii and Gavriil, to Irkutsk, where they were to attend proper school. The boys traveled under the escort of their grandmother and uncle Stephan. Stephan was accompanied by his Unalaskan wife Melania (Melaniia Grigor'ievna Molchanov, born 1811 at Unalaska) and their infant son Feodosii (born 1831).

Stephan, at Unalaska, served as sub-deacon in his brother's church. Now, he was to complete his ecclesiastical training in Irkutsk. In 1833, Stephan was assigned as priest to the church at Kachug near Irkutsk (and Anga). But almost immediately he volunteered for service in northern Kamchatka, at Lesnoi and Palana, as his *matushka* Melania "pined away without the sea." She never saw the sea again, though: she died en route, in Yakutia, at Vitim. Little Feodosii accompanied his father to Kamchatka and soon acted as his interpreter, having rapidly learned the Itel'men (Kamchadal) and Koriak languages from his playmates.

The two brothers met only three more times, when St. Innocent, as bishop and then archbishop, visited the remote corner of Kamchatka where Stephan served as parish priest and missionary. On one of these visits St. Innocent persuaded Stephan to let his only child, Feodosii, come to Sitka and attend the newly established seminary there. The boy drowned on 26 August 1847, together with eight other seminarians and their small craft navigation instructor on a fishing trip to Katlian Bay.

In 1834 Fr. Ioann left Unalaska. Initially he was reassigned to Kodiak, but his orders were changed before he could take up residence there. He went to Sitka instead, where he replaced Fr. Sokolov at the Novoarkhangel'sk Church of St. Michael. His service as Unalaska parish priest was recognized by his superiors and in 1835 he received the award of the Order of St. Anna (3d degree), which elevated his descendants to the status of hereditary nobility of the Russian Empire.[3]

Nevertheless, Fr. Ioann wished fervently to return to Russia. Finally, the permission to leave Alaska was granted in 1838. He sent his wife, the youngest boy, Alexander, and the three elder girls, Catherine, Olga and Paraskeva, home to Irkutsk via Okhotsk. He was to proceed to St. Petersburg by way of a voyage around the world. Little "Kusha" (Fekla) traveled with him. His personal account of the voyage apparently perished with his other papers in the fire at the Monastery of the Savior in Yakutsk in 1858, but even as metropolitan he occasionally recalled the stopovers in exotic places: Hawaii, Tahiti, and Rio de Janeiro especially appealed to him.

In St. Petersburg and then in Moscow, Fr. Ioann was busy with Church authorities, getting acquainted with Metropolitan Filaret, and with preparation for publication of a number of scholarly works and of translations into, and compositions in, the Aleut language.

But unexpectedly, a heavy blow fell. While preparing to travel to Moscow in January 1840, he received news that his wife had died in Irkutsk on 24 November 1839. Little Alexander, too, died that same year.[4]

His first response was to ask for permission to return to Irkutsk to take care of his motherless children. This was not to be. Metropolitan Filaret began to press him to enter the monastic life. Fr. Ioann initially resisted this and accepted reassignment to America as archpriest and dean of clergy. He attempted to resolve his spiritual struggle on a pilgrimage to the holy sites of Kiev, the cradle of Russian Orthodoxy, and in long talks with the spiritual mentors at the Kiev Ecclesiastical Academy, the most famous theological school in Russia. Metropolitan Filaret continued to press him, but he steadfastly refused, saying that his children needed him. The metropolitan then took matters in his own hands and set in motion the machinery to ensure education for all Veniaminov's children at state cost. Finally, exactly one year after the death of his wife, on her name day, the feast of St. Catherine, Fr. Ioann consented to become a monk. He was tonsured on 29 November 1840 in the Trinity Monastery of St. Sergius (where he eventually ended his days) by Metropolitan Filaret himself, and took the name of Innokentii to honor the first Bishop of Irkutsk and patron saint of that city, St. Innocent (Kulchitskii).[5] It should be noted that to the end of his days, St. Innocent denied the common assumption that it was the death of his wife that motivated him to accept tonsure.

The motivation came from elsewhere. It was not only Metropolitan Filaret who urged such a course of action. Under the personal direction of Emperor Nicholas I, the Kamchatka Diocese, previously abolished, was reconstituted and renamed the Diocese of Kamchatka, the Kurile and Aleutian Islands. Also upon personal recommendation of the emperor, newly tonsured Hieromonk Innokentii, immediately elevated to the rank of archimandrite, was appointed to serve as bishop of the new diocese.

Before setting out on his second voyage to America, St. Innocent formally petitioned the government for education of his two remaining sons in Vifaniia Seminary near St. Petersburg and of his daughters (with the exception of Catherine, who was about to be married in Irkutsk to a young clergyman) in special institutions for girls. Catherine and her young husband, Il'ia Petelin, came with St. Innocent to Alaska, where Petelin served as the first resident priest at Nushagak, then at Kodiak, and later settled on the Okhotsk Sea littoral where he served both the Russian settlers and the Even people. Paraskeva became a nun, taking the name of Poliksenia. Her father corresponded with her to the end of his days. The other two girls both married clergymen, in St. Petersburg. Olga was widowed at the age of twenty-three and died the same year, leaving an infant daughter, Nataliia Muzovskii. Fekla, married to Konstantin Molchanov, had a daughter, Anna, born in 1858. Later, she became an alcoholic and returned to Irkutsk.[6]

The eldest son, Innokentii, was expelled from the seminary. A failure, apparently a gambler, and in debt, he became a sore trial to his father. He begged to be permitted to become a priest, but his father forbade it: he did not want his son to become a failed and unworthy clergyman. Eventually, St. Innocent even recommended that he be sent to the army on the Caucasus front in the hope of straightening out his life. But there, too, he failed. Eventually, he was jailed, served several years of his

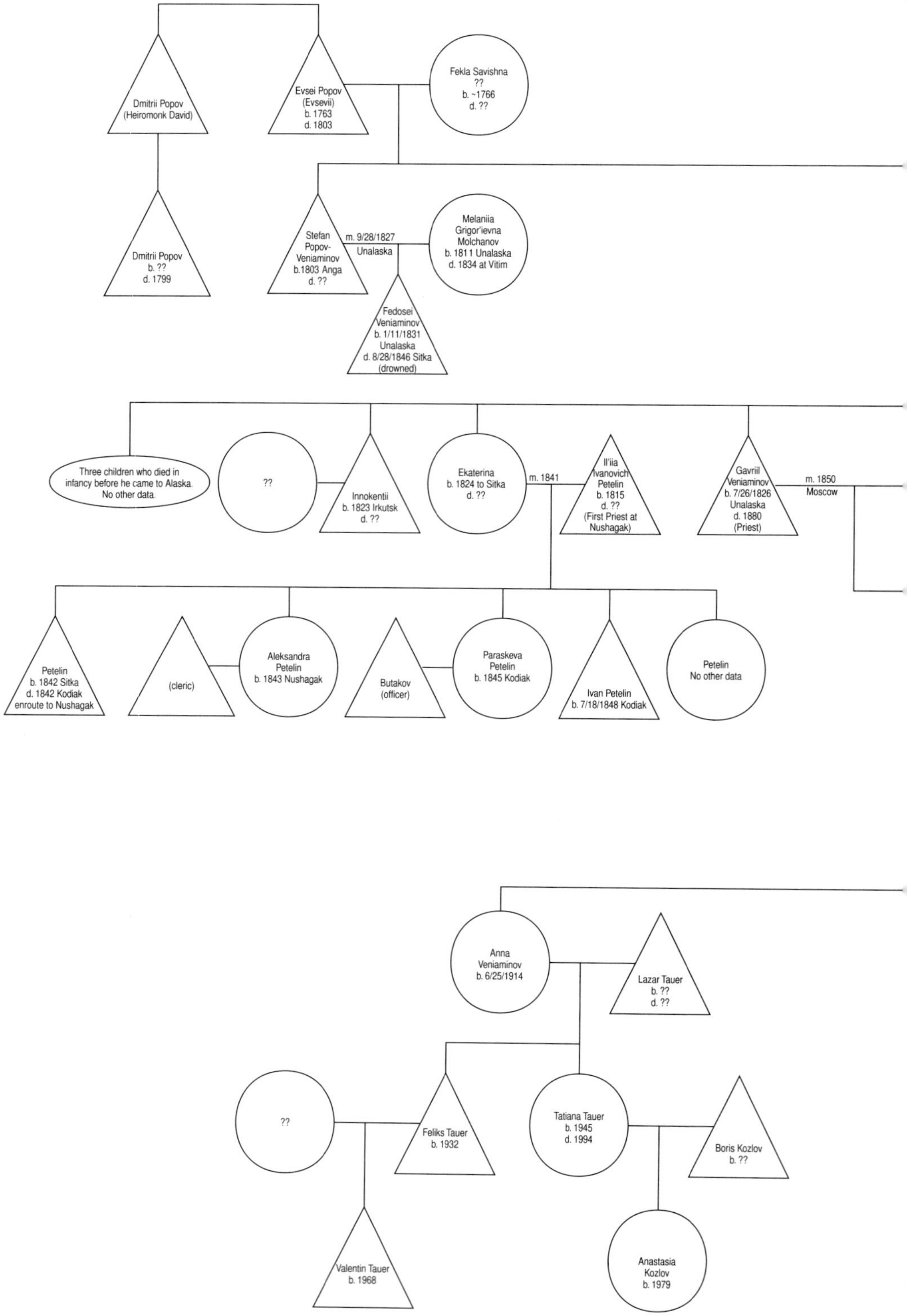
Dmitrii Popov (Heiromonk David)
Evsei Popov (Evsevii) b. 1763 d. 1803
Fekla Savishna ?? b. ~1766 d. ??
Dmitrii Popov b. ?? d. 1799
Stefan Popov-Veniaminov b.1803 Anga d. ??
m. 9/28/1827 Unalaska
Melaniia Grigor'ievna Molchanov b. 1811 Unalaska d. 1834 at Vitim
Fedosei Veniaminov b. 1/11/1831 Unalaska d. 8/28/1846 Sitka (drowned)
Three children who died in infancy before he came to Alaska. No other data.
??
Innokentii b. 1823 Irkutsk d. ??
Ekaterina b. 1824 to Sitka d. ??
m. 1841
Il'iia Ivanovich Petelin b. 1815 d. ?? (First Priest at Nushagak)
Gavriil Veniaminov b. 7/26/1826 Unalaska d. 1880 (Priest)
m. 1850 Moscow
Petelin b. 1842 Sitka d. 1842 Kodiak enroute to Nushagak
(cleric)
Aleksandra Petelin b. 1843 Nushagak
Butakov (officer)
Paraskeva Petelin b. 1845 Kodiak
Ivan Petelin b. 7/18/1848 Kodiak
Petelin No other data
Anna Veniaminov b. 6/25/1914
Lazar Tauer b. ?? d. ??
??
Feliks Tauer b. 1932
Tatiana Tauer b. 1945 d. 1994
Boris Kozlov b. ??
Valentin Tauer b. 1968
Anastasia Kozlov b. 1979

St. Innocent's Family Tree

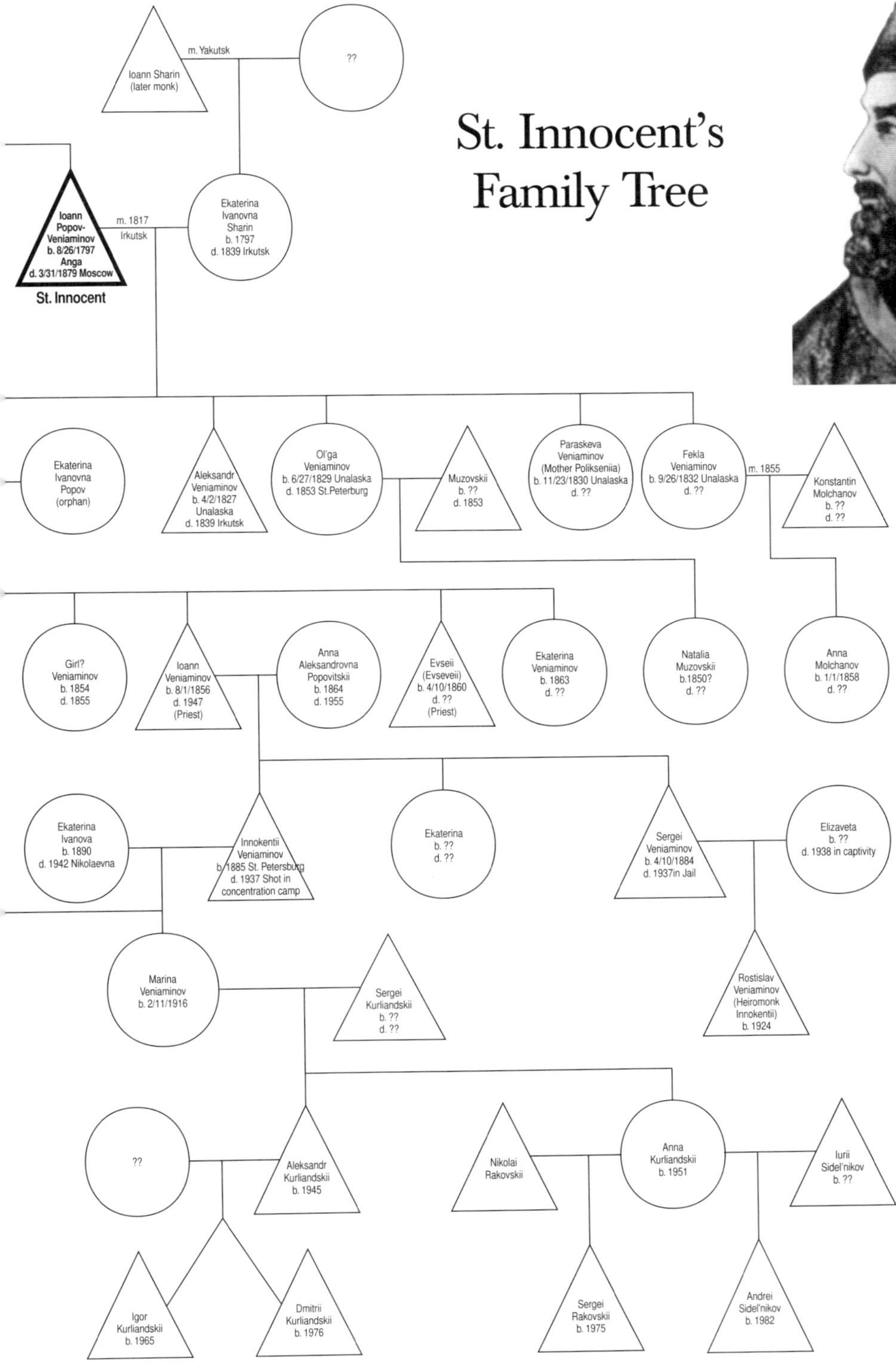

sentence,[7] and was released before his term was up only upon petition of his father, whose service to the state gained Innokentii a reduced sentence. He had married without letting his father know. St. Innocent spared no effort to learn the identity and whereabouts of his daughter-in-law and assigned funds for her support while Innokentii was in jail. He supported Innokentii materially, but placed control over the funds in other hands, as Innokentii would let everything slip away. When Olga willed a sum of 1000 rubles to her sister, the nun Poliksenia, St. Innocent begged the latter to give the money to her relatively poor sister Catherine, but most of it to her brother Innokentii. He never abandoned his wayward son. He constantly urged Gavriil to care for his brother and brother's wife, and was grateful to friends who did not abandon Innokentii.

> I am not disowning him, no, no! Wherever he will be, whoever he will become, I shall always call him my son. . . .If there should be a necessity and it is possible to do so, I personally would attend him in his needs. For Lord's sake, I implore you, take care of him . . . I do not blame anyone . . . if there is blame it is mine. . . . Where is my unhappy son? . . . I never stopped loving him. . . .[8]

St. Innocent's younger surviving son, Gavriil, did finish the seminary and eventually joined his father in Novoarkhangel'sk. Gavriil, it appears, suffered from the fact that he lacked his father's brilliance. In a letter to Gavriil of 22 July 1843, St. Innocent wrote: "It gives me great pleasure that you study well and diligently. Do not complain or fret that you lack swift intellect. All that is ours comes from the Lord. He knows why you were not given great intellectual gifts. But you do have a good heart, and that is worth a thousand times more than intellectual gifts. The Lord did not shortchange you. Watch out and do not bury this precious talent of yours."

Gavriil, by arrangement made by his guardians, married an orphan girl, named Catherine like his mother and elder sister, in Moscow. Later, when Fr. Gavriil served as missionary-priest on Sakhalin Island and in the Amur region, she learned the Southern Tungus languages in order to work with the Negidal and other Tungus-speaking women and earned the respect and affection of her father-in-law.

It is through Gavriil that the Veniaminov family line continued.[9] Gavriil and Catherine Veniaminov had four children. The eldest child died in infancy. Ioann, the eldest surviving son, was born in 1850, his brother Evsevii in 1860, and the only daughter, named Catherine, in 1863.[10]

Both of Gavriil's sons, belonging now to the hereditary nobility, graduated from the Alexander Military School and entered the elite Semeonovskii Guards regiment. Both eventually resigned from military service and became priests. Evsevii was consecrated priest in 1892 and served at the Alexander Nevskii Lavra (monastery) in Khar'kov. Ioann first served in Kovno (modern Lithuania), then, like his brother, in the Khar'kov region, and eventually came to St. Petersburg. There he was appointed as priest to the Tavricheskii Palace and later of the Annichkov Palace and was father-confessor to Dowager Empress Maria Fedorovna. He assisted Ivan Barsukov in the compilation of the first authoritative biography of St. Innocent. He was arrested in the 1920s and spent years in jail. At one point he was in a cell holding 22 men, including four priests and a deacon. At Christmas and New Year's (1928) the incarcerated clergy sang the evening services and were joined by other prisoners. Eventually, he was banished to a remote corner of Russia, where he died in 1947 and was buried in Kashin. Evsevii, too, lived to witness the Communist takeover in Russia. He is obliquely mentioned in a few surviving letters by Ioann G. Veniaminov's wife, Anna (see below). However, his fate is not known at the present time.

Evsevii left no descendants. It may be that he never married. Ioann (Ivan), while still in the army, married Anna Popovitskii in 1882. They had three children, two sons, Sergei (born 1884) and Innokentii (born 1885), and one daughter, Catherine (birth date not known). Both men were shot in 1937 under the Soviet regime. Their sister, Catherine, was still alive in 1955. At this time, we do not know if she ever married or when she died.

Sergei I. Veniaminov is survived by his only son, Rostislav (born 1924), who is now Hieromonk Innokentii and resides in St. Petersburg. Innokentii I. Veniaminov, shot in Kemerovo for alleged conspiracy to organize an uprising of the concentration camp inmates, is survived by two daughters, Anna and Marina. Anna lives in St. Petersburg, Marina in Moscow, Russia. Anna's daughter, Tatiana Tauer, was a famous harpist (she died in 1994) and Tatiana's daughter, Anastasia Kozlov, a violinist, resides in Amsterdam, Netherlands. Marina has a son, Aleksandr Kurliandskii, and daughter Anna. Her four grandchildren also live in Moscow. One grandson, Dr. Igor A. Kurliandskii, a

Above: The elder of St. Innocent's grandsons, Ioann G. Veniaminov, lieutenant in the Semeonovskii Guards Regiment (later a priest) and his bride Anna (Popovitskii), St. Petersburg, ca. 1882.

Below: St. Innocent's great-grandsons (Ioann and Anna Veniaminov's sons) Innokentii and Sergei. Both were political prisoners and shot in 1937 during Stalinist purges in Russia.

Anna A. Veniaminov in her old age, with her granddaughters Marina (Kurliandskaia) and Anna (Tauer), daughters of Innokentii I. Veniaminov. Both are still alive and reside in Russia.

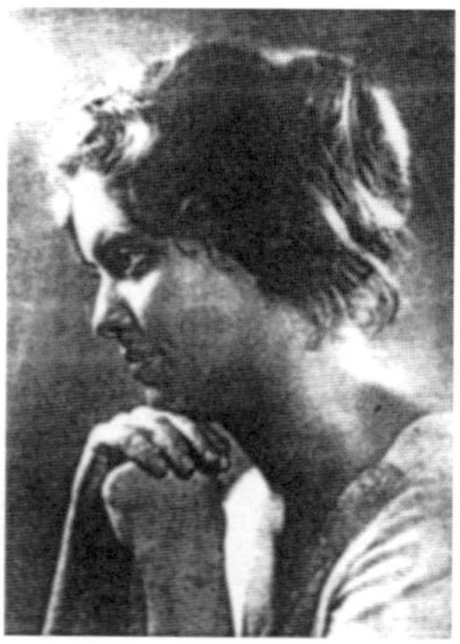

Tat'iana Tauer, Anna's daughter, 1945–1994. A famed harpist.

historian and archivist, is currently working on a new scholarly biography of his illustrious ancestor, St. Innocent, Apostle to Alaska and Siberia.[11]

It is fitting to close this section with an excerpt from the reminiscences of Anna Popovitskii Veniaminov, widow of Fr. Ioann G. Veniaminov, dated in the old fashioned manner 25 February/10 March 1951, four years before her death:

> . . . Dearest Leliushechka, I am sending you my dairy from which you shall learn how long I spent in this world, how my childhood and youth were carefree and happy, I might say, rich, and at the end of my life I found, too, much that was good. I do not wish to complain, but so much was endured, and then with difficulty: hunger, and eviction from living quarters; living in rooms, damp and cold, infested with bedbugs and lice. To get a piece of bread for my poor old dear man or a cup of milk, I mended stockings and underwear for others, and was paid in bread or a bit of milk.
>
> Once again, I do not whine but praise the Lord for everything, as I was taught by my dear old man who himself never complained. . . . While my eyes still see well, I work at whatever I am able to do without glasses, read all sorts of books and newspapers. But most of all I love to read the Holy Bible and the Prophecies of the Holy Prophets. This is the story of my entire life. Before the end comes, I should like to take monastic vows. I shall consult in this my friend who has taken the place of my unforgettable companion Father *baten'ka* who taught me never to complain about anything, be charitable to all and help everyone. Amen!

Notes

1 Sources: Ivan P. Barsukov, *Innokentii, Mitropolit Moskovskii i Kolomenskii po ego sochineniiam, pis'mam i rasskazam sovremennikov* (Moscow: Synod Press, 1883); idem, compiler and editor, *Pis'ma Innokentiia Mitropolita Moskovskago i Kolomenskago 1828-1878*, in 3 volumes (St. Petersburg: Synod Press, 1897, 1898, 1901); A.D. Drizdo and R. V. Kinzhalov, *Russkaia Amerika: Po lichnym vpechatleniiam missionerov, zemleprokhodtsev, moriakov, issledovatelei i drugikh ochevidtsev* (Moscow: Mysl', 1994). Letters of St. Innocent to Kiril Khlebnikov (1824-1836) appear on pp. 151-189 of the latter.

Information on St. Innocent's descendants has been provided in photocopied and typescript copies of documents preserved by the family, courtesy of Dr. Igor A. Kurliandskii, direct descendant of St. Innocent in the female line.

2 For an excellent description of the route to America, see James R. Gibson, *Feeding the Russian Fur Trade. Provisionment of the Okhotsk Seaboard and the Kamchatka Peninsula 1639-1856* (Madison, Milwau-

kee, and London: The University of Wisconsin Press, 1969), chapter 5, "Routes and Carriers," pp. 72-104.

3 He received the Order of St. Anna (2d and 1st degrees) in 1840, in the same year that he was elevated to the status of archpriest.

4 It is possible that St. Innocent's mother, Fekla, also died at that time, as he does not mention her, but only her relatives, in later correspondence. The question of the deaths of St. Innocent's family members requires further research.

5 The Orthodox cathedral in Anchorage is consecrated to St. Innocent of Irkutsk and so is one of the side chapels at the Cathedral of the Holy Ascension of Christ in Unalaska. At the latter, the second chapel, in which the Royal Gate from the church Fr. Ioann built in 1825/1826 is preserved, is consecrated to St. Sergius of Radonezh, founder of the Holy Trinity Monastery where St. Innocent of Alaska and Siberia was tonsured and where his body reposes.

6 It is not clear if Fekla left her well-connected husband or if she was widowed before returning to Irkutsk. Our evidence is a brief mention of "my unhappy daughter" in one of St. Innocent's letters.

7 The crime for which Innokentii I. Veniaminov was jailed is not known.

8 The fate of Innokentii I. Veniaminov and his wife remains unknown. They are not mentioned in the letters dating to the 1860s nor in St. Innocent's will. We assume that Innokentii died childless and before his father.

9 See the genealogical table in this volume.

10 Ekaterina Gavriilovna Veniaminov was educated in St. Petersburg and lived there in the 1880s. Her fate is not known at this point.

11 Dr. Kurliandskii provided copies of documents, letters, and the reminiscences/dairy of Anna Popovitskii Veniaminov which enabled us to partially reconstruct the history of St. Innocent's descendants. Dr. Kurliandskii is a participant in the international conference *Ioann Veniaminov–His Contribution to Arctic Social Sciences*, University of Alaska Fairbanks, 5-7 December 1997.

Innokentii (Ioann Veniaminov), Metropolitan of Moscow and Kolomna, 1868–1879.

Photo taken at the Holy Trinity–St. Sergius of Radonezh Monastery by F. Osipov, exact date unknown, but not long before the Metropolitan's death. Courtesy of A. Sergius Larre, Zagorsk, Russia.

:XIV: The Final Rest

Metropolitan Innokentii died on Holy Saturday, 31 March 1879, at 2:45 a.m. By eleven that morning the great bell of the Moscow Kremlin began to toll the archpastor's passing. Death overtook St. Innocent at the Holy Trinity–St. Sergius of Radonezh Monastery. It was here, as a young man, that he took refuge after receiving the news of his wife's death in Irkutsk. He was here, when his mentor and friend, Filaret, as Metropolitan of Moscow, urged him to consider entering monastic life. It was here that in the fall of 1840 he finally received monastic tonsure.

His body was interred in the Church of the Holy Spirit, next to Filaret's resting place. On the sarcophagus, the following words were inscribed:

> May your episcopal service be remembered by the Lord God in his kingdom always, now and forever, into ages of ages.

On the top rested a crucifix and under it there was the inscription:

> Through the prayers of St. Innocent [of Irkutsk], Lord Jesus Christ, Our God, have mercy on us.

It is said that in the course of the persecution of the Church by the Soviet regime, the remains of St. Filaret and St. Innocent were disinterred and thrown into a pit. Recovered in more recent times (St. Innocent's remains were recognized by the tall stature), they were restored to the sarcophagi and returned to the Church of the Holy Spirit.[1]

Metropolitan Innocent recognized that the end was near and prepared himself by having the canon and prayers for the dying read continuously at his bedside. As early as December 1869, however, knowing that his eyesight was failing, he prepared his will:

Above: Church of the Holy Ghost in Zagorsk, site of St. Innocent's tomb.

Right: The combined tomb of St. Innocent, right, and St. Filaret, left.

Photos by Stanton H. Patty, from *The Alaska Journal*, v. 2, no. 2, Spring 1972, pp. 35-37. Reproductions used by permission of Alaska Northwest Publishing Co. and Mr. Robert Henning.

In the name of the Father and the Son and the Holy Spirit. Though my state of health is rather satisfactory considering my advanced age, my eyesight is growing ever weaker and blindness threatens. Therefore, I decided to commit to paper, while I still can see what I am writing, my testament which is to take effect at my death.

First, I offer thanks to my God and Lord, who always is benevolent to me and protected me on all my path!

1) I beg and implore all and everyone whom I have offended, hurt or to whom I caused sadness, by word or by deed, to forgive me fully and forever for our Savior's sake; and I, too, for His sake, fully and forever forgive each and everyone who at some time or other caused me grief, or offense, or hurt by word or by deed. I also forgive all my debtors who are unable without hardship to redeem such debts.

2) My sinful body I ask to be interred in the St. Sergius Lavra in the common cemetery for the brothers, within the palisade. Of course, this applies only if I still will be the abbot. Otherwise, I am to be buried as the authorities decide.

3) I beg and implore not to hold any speeches or eulogies either before, during, or after my burial. If it was hard to me to hear pan-

egyrics in the weak light of Truth which guided me during my lifetime, how much should I suffer hearing unearned praise there where the Truth is Supreme? If, however, someone decides to say a few words, please let him take as his text: "The Lord guides the footsteps of a man," stating who I was and where I did what I did, to the Glory of God, but omitting any words of [personal] praise.

4) Do not erect any monuments over my body, except a simple cast iron plate with a simple and brief inscription.

5) My entire estate I bequeath to my sole heir, my son the Archpriest Gabriel [Gavriil] Veniaminov. None of my daughters nor their children, have a right to demand anything from him out of my estate.

6) Of the remaining panageias, one of them of the Annunciation, on stone, is to be sent to the Cathedral of the Annunciation in Blagoveshchensk, and the other, also on stone, of the Theotokos of the Sign [Znameniia], to the cathedral in the former Russian colonies in America [Sitka].

7) The desk clock I bequeath to my grandson John [Ioann], and my gold pocket watch to my grandson Eusebius [Evsevii] Veniaminov. From any cash that is left, up to five hundred rubles are to be given to children of my sisters and relatives of my mother, at my heir's discretion.

Note

1 This story, told widely in Russia today, may be apocryphal. The Church of the Holy Spirit is now undergoing extensive restoration, and the relics of the two famous Metropolitans of Moscow and Kolomna, Filaret and Innokentii, are temporarily reposing in the Trapeznaia Church of the monastery.

Tropar to Saint Innocent, Equal to the Apostles, Enlightener of Alaska and Asia

You evangelized the Northern Peoples of Alaska and Asia/
Proclaiming the Gospel of Christ to the Natives in their own tongues/
O Holy Hierarch Father Innocent/
Enlightener of the Aleutians and Apostle to America/
Whose ways were ordered by the Lord/
Pray to the Lord for the salvation of our souls//
In His Heavenly Kingdom.

Glorified a Saint of the
Russian Orthodox Church
6 October 1977

Icon of St. Innocent by Byron Birdsall.

:XV: The Legacy

The legacy of St. Innocent in Alaska is manifest above all in the many Orthodox parishes that exist today, from the Athabaskan village of Nikolai on the Upper Kuskokwim, to the large Yup'ik communities on the Lower Yukon and Kuskokwim Rivers, among the Dena'ina of Cook Inlet and Upper Alaska Peninsula, the Chugach of Prince William Sound, the Alutiiq, the Aleut, and the Tlingit communities of southeastern Alaska. Orthodox art flourishes and Orthodox music is being composed in Native languages. St. Herman's Theological Seminary in Kodiak has predominantly Alaska Native students. As St. Innocent foresaw, many Americans of different origins embrace the Orthodox faith.

In Yakutia, the Year of St. Innocent is being celebrated with the full support of the Sakha Republic government. In addition to two international conferences, research into St. Innocent's role as a spiritual leader in nineteenth-century Yakutia is being undertaken. St. Innocent is being remembered as the father of Yakut written literature. The works he sponsored in the Yakut language are being reprinted, and a proposal is being advanced to reprint the St. Innocent literary corpus in toto. In Kamchatka, the St. Innocent's Third Lecture Series, an international conference, took place this September.[1]

Throughout Russia, St. Innocent has become a patron saint of spiritual and moral revitalization and regeneration.

Artists in Russia, America and Europe find inspiration for their work in his life. Representation of St. Innocent in iconography in the few years since his glorification in 1977 is very rich and the treasury of icons of St. Innocent, Apostle to Alaska and Siberia, is growing with each day. We are proud to have in this exhibit what is probably the first icon painted of the newly glorified Saint, by the late Aleut self-taught artist Agafangel Stepetin of Unalaska, along with the icons by such accomplished iconographers as Byron Birdsall and his daughter, Courtenay E.

Birdsall, of Anchorage, Alaska. A beaded icon by Eleanor Naumoff of Old Harbor, Kodiak Island, was created by the artist especially for this exhibit. A number of copies of icons representing St. Innocent by American, Russian, and European iconographers are included. The life and story of St. Innocent have also inspired a number of secular works by such artists as Rie Munoz of Juneau, Alaska, Ray Hudson of Middlebury, Vermont, Dorothy Hook of Brockport, Pennsylvania, and Dimitrii Philemonof of St. George, Alaska, among others. A selection is included in this exhibit.

St. Innocent's name is invoked in Orthodox churches throughout the world, but he is honored also by members of other faiths. In Alaska, he was never forgotten and until recently his memory was preserved in the villages by word of mouth. In 1975, Fr. Ismail Gromoff of Unalaska composed this story for the children he taught:

The late Father Ismail Gromoff, Pastor of the Church of the Holy Ascension of Christ, Unalaska.
Photo by L. Black, 1976.

A Story About Father Veniaminov

by Father Ismail Gromoff[2]

Did he think of his children, our father, in his great age and blindness? Did he remember us living here on our green island?

Ivan Veniaminov was born in Russia in 1797. His father died when he was young, and he was raised by his uncle. When he was nine he went to the church school where he stayed for eleven years.

In 1817 Veniaminov married. In 1821 he became a priest. Why did he come to Unalaska?

In 1823 the church asked someone to move to Alaska. No one would do it. Then Veniamonov heard about the Aleuts and how they were devoted to prayer and to the Word of God.

With his mother, his wife, his son, and his brother he left Russia in 1823. He reached Unalaska in 1824. His first work was to rebuild the church. He taught the Aleuts to build and carve and together they made a great church to the glory of the Ascension of the Lord. This church was opened 150 years ago.

He traveled in baidarkas to many villages many times. We know that he went to Akun at least four times.

He learned the Aleut language. He showed us how to write our language. He recorded our early ways so that we would remember them. After living here ten years he left us.

He went to Sitka. He became Bishop. He taught other priests; Netzvetov and Shaishnikoff were among the most important. He returned to Russia. He became Metropolitan.

He helped us when he was here and after he left us.

The last day of March 1879 was cold at Unalaska. The rain and the wind blew around the church and the town. We did not know it then but Veniaminov had fallen asleep in God that morning.

Did he think of his children, our father, in his great age and blindness? Did he remember us living here on our green island? Here in this place we would never forget him.

[1] Lectures dedicated to Innokentii, Metropolitan of Moscow and Kolomna, were held regularly in the Russian Far East under the auspices of the Imperial Geographic Society before the revolution in 1917. They were reinstituted in 1991. The second series was held in 1993.

[2] From *Aleut for Beginners* (Unalaska City School: Aleut Language Instruction, 1975), 33–34.

Donors and Exhibit Support

The Alaska State Veniaminov Bicentennial Committee expresses deeply felt gratitude for support received from individuals and organizations without which this exhibit could not have become a reality.

Individuals

His Beatitude Theodosius, Metropolitan of All America and Canada

His Eminence, Michael J. Kaniecki, S.J., Bishop of Fairbanks

Dr. Marvin Andresen and Dr. Patricia Andresen, Fairbanks
Dr. Charlotte Basham, Fairbanks
Dr. Lydia Black, Fairbanks
Donald and Mary Ann Borshert
Daniel and Sharon Boyette, Anchorage
Michael and Margaret Carey, Anchorage
Dr. James Cerney, Fairbanks
Dr. Alyce Cheska, Illinois
Dr. Kerry Feldman, Anchorage
Dr. and Mrs. Michael Gaffney, Fairbanks
Mr. and Mrs. David Gregory, Unalaska
Dr. Susan Grigg, Fairbanks
Mark and Midori Hanus, Oregon
Dr. Susan M. Henrichs, Fairbanks
Mrs. Elizabeth Howe, in memory of her mother Dorothy Eaton
Mr. Robert Juetner, Chugiak
Dr. and Mrs. P. Kamath, Florida
Dr. James M. Kari, Fairbanks
Dr. Judith S. Kleinfeld, Fairbanks
The late Dean Kohlhoff, and Nancy Kohlhoff, Indiana
Dr. Michael Krauss and Dr. Jane Krauss, Fairbanks
Joseph and Gretchen Lake, Fairbanks
Dinah W. Larsen, Oregon
Dr. Margaret Lee, Fairbanks
Dr. Jeff Leer, Fairbanks
Dr. Kent Lightfoot, California
Mrs. Tamara Lincoln, Fairbanks

Mr. Denby Lloyd, Anchorage
Mr. Thomas E. Lux, Rhode Island
Dr. Owen Mason, Fairbanks
Mr. James Moody, Fairbanks
Dr. Phyllis Morrow, Fairbanks
Ms. Claire Murphy, Fairbanks
Vera Nevzuroff, Atka
Mrs. Alice Petrivelli, Anchorage
Ms. Patricia J. Petrivelli, Anchorage
Dr. Victor B. Petrov, Washington, D.C.
Dr. Richard A. Pierce, Fairbanks
Mrs. Christine Riordan, Florida
Ms. Mary Schultheis, Anchorage
Richard and Jo Scott, Fairbanks
Mrs. Jane Arliss Sturgulewski, Anchorage
Roe and Carol Sturgulewski, Seward
Mr. Serge Suleimani, Fairbanks and Magadan
Mrs. Candace Waugaman, Fairbanks
Mrs. Beatrice Wenger, Switzerland
Dr. and Mrs. William Wood, Fairbanks
Dr. Richard and Mrs. Nathalie Woodbury, Massachusetts
Miss Marilyn Zupan, Fairbanks

Organizations and Business Enterprises

A.L.E.U.T. Tours, Unalaska
Afognak Native Corporation
AK Permanent Capital Management Co., Anchorage
The Aleut Corporation, Anchorage
Aleutian/Pribilof Islands Association, Inc., Anchorage
Aleutian and Pribilof Islands Restitution Trust, Anchorage
American Association for the Advancement of Science, Arctic Division Executive Committee
APICDA Joint Ventures, Inc., Juneau
AT&T, Anchorage
Atxam Corporation, Atka
Birch, Horton, Bittner, Inc., Anchorage
Calista Corporation, Anchorage
Cook Inlet Historical Society, Anchorage
Cook Inlet Region, Inc.
Corporation of the Catholic Bishop, Anchorage
Fort Ross Interpretive Association, Inc., California
Joukowsky Family Foundation, New York and Rhode Island
K&L Services, Anchorage
National Bank of Alaska

Ounalashka Corporation
J.C. Penney, Fairbanks
PolarConsult Alaska, Inc. Anchorage
Powerhouse Construction Services, Inc., Fairbanks
Rotary Club of Fairbanks
Ryan Lode Mines, Fairbanks
St. George Tanaq Corporation, Anchorage
Saint John Orthodox Cathederal, Anchorage
St. Nicholas Church of Atka
Seven Seas Fishing Company, Seattle, Washington
Society of Jesus, Alaska
Spacemark, Inc., Colorado
Smithsonian Institution Press, Washington, D.C.
Tanana Yukon Historical Society, Fairbanks
City of Unalaska, Unalaska
University of Alaska Fairbanks, Office of the Provost
University of Edinburgh, United Kingdom

Support by the Alaska Humanities Forum in the form of a grant is gratefully acknowledged. Special thanks go to Reeve Aleutian Airways and PenAir for providing free transportation for the exhibit and accompanying personnel and to Alaska Airlines for transporting the exhibit at reduced cargo rates.

The following individuals have contributed their talents, work, and effort: Mr. Iliodor Philemonof, President, Tanaq Corporation of St. George, suggested the exhibit title; Dr. M. Pamela Bumsted, Fairbanks, established electronic communications; Glen R. J. Mules, webmaster and director of systems, publishes the permanent electronic archives and exhibition (www.oca.org), contributed by the Orthodox Church in America; James W. Cook prepared the computerized geneaology chart; Martin Gutoski prepared the maps; Dr. Katherine L. Arndt edited the catalog text and Dixon J. Jones, Rasmuson Library, UAF, designed the catalog; UAF personnel who went beyond the call of duty helping in various ways with the preparation of the exhibit are Mrs. Tracie Cogdill, Department of Anthropology, Mrs. Bonnie Kleven, Purchasing, Mr. Nathan George, Rasmuson Library, Accounting. Mrs. Alice Petrivelli, Mrs. Sharon Boyette (Aleutians East Borough, Anchorage), Rev. and Mrs. Young (Sitka), and Mrs. Candace Waugaman (Fairbanks) and Mr. and Mrs. Gregory (Unalaska) volunteered assistance in fund raising; Mr. Richard Veazey, Alaska and Polar Regions Department, Rasmuson Library, and his staff are responsible for most of the photographic reproductions used in the exhibit.

Contributors of exhibit materials are Mrs. Barbara S. Smith, Anchorage; Fr. Eugene Bourdukofsky, Sitka; Holy Trinity Monastery, Jordanville, New York; Brotherhood of St. Innocent, Apostle to Alaska and Siberia, Moscow; Dr.Oleg Bychkov and Mr. Vladimir Guliaev, Irkutsk; Dr. Egor Shishigin, University of Sakha Republic (Yakutia), Mirnyi Campus; Mrs. N.S. Ertiukova, Director, State Museums of the Sakha Republic (Yakutia); E.P. Guliaeva, Sakha (Yakutia) National Library, Sakha (Yakutia) State Archive, Yakutsk; Dr. Aleksei A. Istomin, Institute of Ethnography, Academy of Sciences of Russia, Moscow; Katerina Solovyeva Wessels, Anchorage; Aleksei A. Savel'iev, Institute of Oriental Studies, University of St. Petersburg, Rare Books; St. Petersburg Public Library; Victor P. Zakharov, BAN (Library of Russian Academy of Sciences, St. Petersburg); Ms. Molly Molloy, Hoover Institution, Stanford University; Kodiak Historical Society; Fr. Michael Oleksa, Dean, St. Herman's Theological Seminary, Kodiak; Dr. Michael Krauss, Director, ANLC, UAF; Dr. Allan Urbanic, Slavic Bibliographer, University of California, Berkeley; the National Diet Library, Tokyo, Japan, and Dr. Akasofu, Director, Geophysical Institute, UAF; Mrs. Gloria Fisher, ArtWorks, Fairbanks; Linda Cook, National Park Service, Alaska Region, Anchorage; Mr. Gary Gauthier, Superintendent, Sitka National Historical Park; the Church of the Holy Ascension of Christ, Unalaska.

Reproductions of paintings of California Missions by the late Chesley Bonestell are courtesy Space Art International, Chevy Chase, Maryland.

Dr. Igor A. Kurliandskii, Institute of Russian History, Academy of Sciences of Russia, Moscow, direct descendant of St. Innocent, provided invaluable data on Veniaminov family history and on the fate of St. Innocent's family.

Very special thanks go to the artists whose selflessly donated works of art immeasurably enriched this exhibit: Byron Birdsall and his daughter Courtenay Birdsall of Anchorage, and Ray Hudson of Middlebury, Vermont, formerly of Unalaska.